NATIONAL GEOGRAPHIC DIRECTIONS

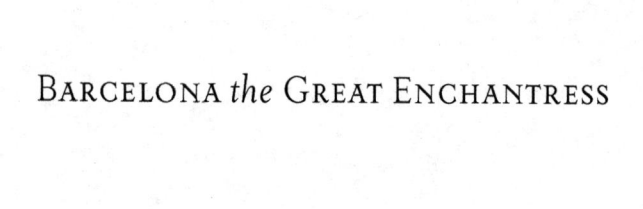

BARCELONA *the* GREAT ENCHANTRESS

Barcelona
the Great
Enchantress

Robert Hughes

NATIONAL GEOGRAPHIC DIRECTIONS

NATIONAL GEOGRAPHIC
Washington, D.C.

Published by the National Geographic Society
1145 17th Street, N.W., Washington, D.C. 20036-4688

Text copyright © 2004 Robert Hughes
Map copyright © 2004 National Geographic Society
Photography Credits: PAGE 13 Ramon Manent/CORBIS; PAGE 43 Andrea Jemolo/CORBIS;
PAGE 118 Patrick Ward/CORBIS; PAGE 122 CORBIS; PAGE 129 Branguli/ngsimages.com; PAGE 144
Jose Fuste Rage/CORBIS; PAGE 146 Mark Segal/Panoramic Images/National Geographic
Image Collection.

Library of Congress Cataloging-in-Publication Data
Hughes, Robert, 1938-
  Barcelona, the Great Enchantress / Robert Hughes.
    p. cm. -- (National Geographic directions)
  ISBN 0-7922-6794-X (hardcover)
  1. Barcelona (Spain)--Civilization. 2. Barcelona (Spain)--Description and travel. 3. Hughes, Robert,
1938---Homes and haunts--Spain--Barcelona. 4. Arts, Spanish--Spain--Barcelona. 5. Architecture--
Spain--Barcelona. 6. Barcelona (Spain)--Buildings, structures, etc. I. Title. II. Series.
  DP402.B265H87 2004
  946'.72--dc22
                                                  2004006082

One of the world's largest nonprofit scientific and educational organizations, the National Geographic
Society was founded in 1888 "for the increase and diffusion of geographic knowledge." Fulfilling this
mission, the Society educates and inspires millions every day through its magazines, books, television
programs, videos, maps and atlases, research grants, the National Geographic Bee, teacher workshops,
and innovative classroom materials. The Society is supported through membership dues, charitable
gifts, and income from the sale of its educational products. This support is vital to National
Geographic's mission to increase global understanding and promote conservation of our planet
through exploration, research, and education.

For more information, please call 1-800-NGS LINE (647-5463), write to the Society at the above
address, or visit the Society's Web site at www.nationalgeographic.com.

Interior design by Melissa Farris

Printed in the U.S.A.

*To Daisy, who loves the highest
when she sees it.*

BARCELONA *the* GREAT ENCHANTRESS

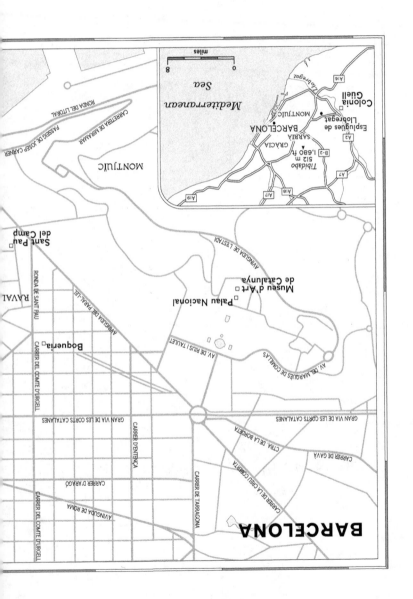

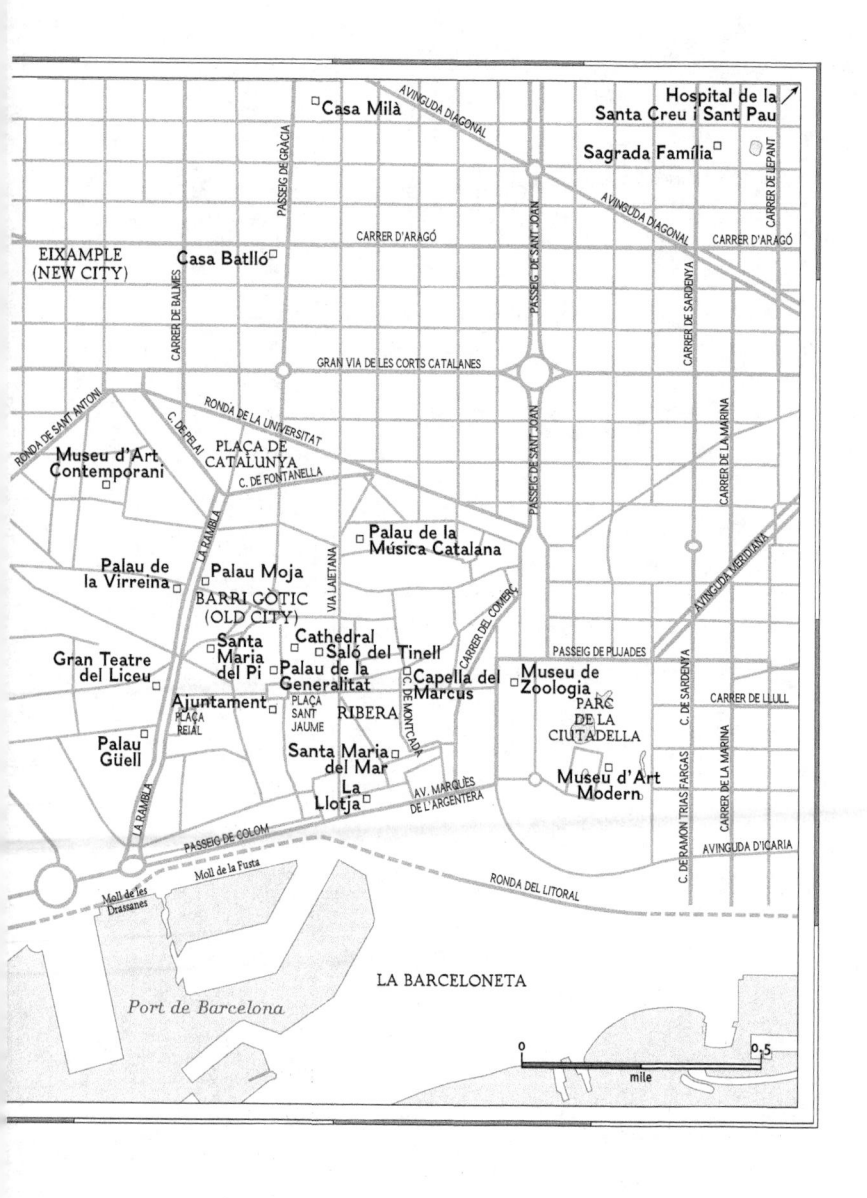

ONE

I FIRST WENT TO BARCELONA NEARLY FOUR DECADES AGO, in 1966. This happened because I was an opinionated and poorly informed loudmouth. I spoke little Spanish and no Catalan, but at a party in London, under the influence of various stimulants, I had been holding forth on the subject of the great and long-dead Catalan architect Antoni Gaudí. I had some theories, entirely cribbed from French writers, about the surrealist affinities of Gaudí's work. (In fact it has no surrealist affinities of any discernible kind. Indeed it is utterly and fundamentally opposed to everything the surrealists believed in and tried to propagate, but well, hell, it was the swinging sixties in London and you didn't need proof. Bullshit would do.) As I warmed to my theme, or themes, if you could call them that, I observed that a foreign-looking man was watching me and listening, quizzically. He was youngish, but older than me, about thirty. He was very close shaven but had the swarthy look of a Gypsy. His pomaded hair, long at the back, curled somewhat greasily over a stiffish and striped collar. He had a brown suit, tobacco colored and of extreme though somehow dated elegance, the jacket tubular and tightly buttoned, in the utmost contrast to the flowing and flopping garments or patched self-embroidered jeans worn by the other men in the room. A handmade Turkish handkerchief hung negligently from his breast pocket. His shirt was formal and his shoes had clearly been handmade, too, smoothly encasing his small and birdlike feet like shining purses. He was smoking an unfiltered Players—about the fiftieth of the day, I would later come to realize.

"It is good to meet a fan of Gaudí in England," he said in a dense growling accent, "even if you know so little about him."

And this was how I came to meet the man who before the evening was out became my friend, and forty years later is still my dearest and oldest one: the Catalan sculptor Xavier Corberó. Xavier forgave me for prating about a subject of which I knew nothing, since I could hardly be blamed for not having been to

Barcelona. "Very few people have," he said, a trifle dismissively, implying that the world is full of fools anyway. But he was not going to let me continue to be a fool, and the only way around that was to ensure that I should actually see the works of Gaudí, not just the Sagrada Família—the unfinished temple that everyone mentioned as the epitome of his work, but which in his view was by no means its summa—but a number of other buildings by him as well. He reeled off their names in his sharply clacking Catalan accent, leaving me quite nonplussed: I might call myself an art critic, and in point of fact I did, but I had never heard of any of them. The same for the various other Catalan architects of the art nouveau period (about 1870-1920) whose names Xavier let fall, and the artists, and so on and so forth. Clearly, there was a whole bunch of stuff just down there, under the shadow of the Pyrenees, of which I was quite virginally ignorant. And Xavier wanted me to know about it; not in the spirit of an art dealer promoting his fondest find, but because, as a serious Catalan—a creature not to be confused with a normal Spaniard—he could not endure the spectacle of someone else's ignorance of his own *patria chica*.

So I went. And shortly afterward, returned. And then, the next spring, went again. I was hooked and couldn't stay away. Once I lived in a peculiar, once grand but now somewhat ramshackle hotel at the foot of the road up whose middle the electric tramway ran, clattering and groaning, to Tibidabo, the vantage point from which the whole plain of Barcelona could be seen spreading below; this hotel, though much lower than Tibidabo, had a domed mirador on the roof sumptuously ornamented with 1900-style mosaics, in which one could sit, look at the city, and dream on a hot day. It seemed to have no other clients (at least I never saw one) and its room rate was somewhat less than ten dollars a day. The bed sagged and the faucet spat a thin stream of boiling brown water. It was, I thought, heaven.

But mostly I stayed in Xavier's house. It was not in town. It was a country *masia,* in a village named Esplugües de Llobregat, which had not yet been absorbed by the southerly expansion of Barcelona itself. (Today it almost has, but Xavier owns most of the cobbled street the home stands in, so the place is in no danger. It's just a completely unexpected, and unpredictable, oasis of the seventeenth and eighteenth centuries in the middle of the twenty-first—a time warp in brick and stucco.) Named the Can Cargol (House of the Snail), it stands on a back road above the village. Esplugües in Catalan means "caves"—it comes from the Latin *speluncas*—and that is what the Can Cargol has in its basement: an extended, twisting series of grottoes dug deep into the hillside for reasons of storage and, perhaps originally, defense, by farmers who owned the area in Roman times. Possibly these subterranean windings reminded people of the secret labyrinth of a snail shell, and so named the house. But even when I was staying in the Can Cargol in the '60s, I never ventured to properly explore these catacombs, being cravenly afraid of spiders and darkness. Only God, or perhaps Pluto, deity of the underworld, knows with any certainty what is down there. One of the caves has, or at least had, an enormous printing press in it, a greasy dusty Moloch of a machine dating from the mid-nineteenth century, on which some long-dead radical Catalanist may well have run off anti-Carlist tracts in bygone days. For years Xavier and his friends, including myself, drank an excellent red wine of which someone in Penedes had given him hundreds of bottles: Since he had not bothered to have storage racks made, those bottles were simply dumped, higgledy-piggledy, on the earthen floor of the catacomb, where their labels were nibbled away to illegibility over the years by rats, mold, and insects.

The Can Cargol was one of the few rustic buildings of its kind left near Barcelona—a splendid example of the structure known, since time immemorial, as a *casa pairal* or patriarchal house. Those who know the early work of the great Catalan painter Joan Miró will know such structures immediately: The house of his childhood depicted in "The Farm," 1922, is one. They have small windows, heavy roofs like thick cakes of terracotta, and walls of a cyclopean thickness, built to keep out centuries of bandits and foul weather. Their roofs project like drooping, angled wings, creating an overriding sense of shelter and enclosure. And their core, spiritual as well as physical, is the *llar de foc,* the fireplace (you could almost translate this as the "lair of the fire")—more like a whole room in itself, where the entire peasant family assembled, always depicted as ranked in order of age from grandparents to infants: a house within a house. Xavier lived in yet another house across the narrow road, to which there was no access except by a key that he refused to have copied, and the lock on the front door of the Can Cargol was of an old-fashioned type which could only be shut with its own key. Synchronizing one's comings and goings with his was, therefore, a complicated business, but most of the time one could at least hope for, if not wholly rely on, the appearance of an elderly and toothless housekeeper who, muttering like the porter in *Macbeth,* would let one in or out.

ONCE I HAD GOT USED TO CATALAN HOURS (NOT AN easy business, in a city where an earlyish dinner meant eating at 10:30), Xavier would drag his guest off to places I know I could hardly find again. Not just the hole-in-the-wall junk shops, or the Gothic churches in which Barcelona is so overpoweringly rich, or the dark restaurants full of noisy *catalanistas*, but real oddities: There was, I distinctly remember, a house for sale which we visited and fantasized about buying and turning into a house of assignation for rich tourists (Xavier seemed to know precisely where the girls would be found). The house was a gloomy gem of 1900 design whose main feature, apart from an abandoned ebony cradle inlaid with ivory, was a magnificent screen bisecting the main *salón*, a glass screen with painted and fired designs and panels inlaid with the iridescent blue wings of Amazonian morpho butterflies, which must have been installed for the pleasure of some *indiano*, as Catalans who went to South America and made fortunes in slaves or coffee were known. Neither of us had any money. We could not buy the place, and today I have no memory of where it was. But it would have made the grandest cathouse in Spain.

In a different vein, there was the subterranean former workshop of Xavier's late father, a metalworker and decorative sculptor of large repute who had turned out massive bronze stair rails for hotels in Boston, towering light fixtures for the Palau Nacional up on Montjuïc, and even a gilt bronze tabernacle for the high altar of the Catedral de Havana: This costly devotional object was shipped off just before the 1959 Cuban revolution, and the elder Corberó's bill was never paid, leaving him with a hatred of Fidel Castro that burned with a hard and gem-like flame until his death. (It did not pass to his son, who remained resolutely apolitical through the 1960s.) The walls of the *taller* were encrusted with layer on layer of the sculptor's molds and models, a collage so thick that you couldn't see the layers below. It was an Aladdin's cave of decorative sculpture, utterly unlike the pure and minimal forms that Xavier was busy shaping from marble in his studio up in Esplugües.

At night there would be restaurants, some rather grand, most of a refined but vernacular sort, serving out the intense, agrestic cooking of the Ampurdan coast and mountains, for which Xavier and his friends, their wives and girlfriends and women colleagues, had a particular liking. Full speed ahead, and don't hold the garlic. If Barcelona had any tourist restaurants then, I don't remember seeing one or eating in it. I do, however, remember the postprandial nightlife, particularly an extraordinary and raddled old music hall on the Paral-lel down by the harborfront, El Molino. Its acts, stage sets, costumes, and dramatis personae seemed not to have changed since the 1930s. Seated in a box framed by sticky-looking green velvet curtains, happily drunk on a kind of sweet bubbly *cava* served by an ancient waiter who resembled the mad grandfather from *The Munsters,* and not understanding a syllable of the dirty-minded Catalan dialogue, I would watch a stereotypical character known as El Anglès, the Englishman, attired in plus fours and a revolting tweed jacket as loud as Evelyn Waugh's, mincing clumsily about the stage twirling a wooden golf club amid roars of approbation from the clientele. What he was saying, I did not know then and dread to think now.

WHERE COULD YOU WISH TO BE MARRIED, IF NOT IN SUCH a city and among such people? I have been married three times, in three places. The first was in 1967, to an Australian, in a Jesuit church on Farm Street in London. The marriage lasted fourteen years, ended in divorce, and was, for the most part, both crazed and miserably unhappy. The second, which also lasted fourteen years, was to an American, in a rustic summerhouse in the painter Robert Motherwell's garden in Connecticut. Bugs and tiny spiders dropped out of the thatch above our heads as we swore to love, honor, and cherish one another, and we were happy for about eight years. But this union, though promising, also failed because, having been faithful to one another all that time, I met someone else who I knew with certainty would be the love of my life: a tall, beautiful artist from Virginia named Doris Downes. The inevitable divorce was neither easy nor pleasant for either me or my wife, and very expensive for me; but by the fall of 2001 it was an acknowledged legal fact, and Doris and I were free (not without misgivings on her part, though with none on mine) to marry. *Third time lucky,* I kept thinking, and so it has turned out to be.

But there was a question. Where to get hitched? It ought not to be in Manhattan, where I lived. Neither Doris nor I is a particularly social animal. Neither of us wanted a fearsomely expensive wedding, and in my post-divorce financial blues almost anything from a New York caterer beyond a sausage on a stick and a can of beer seemed extravagant. In any case, post-9/11 Manhattan did not feel like a jolly place to tie the knot. But the clincher was that, with three previous wedding receptions between us, neither Doris nor I felt up to shouldering the quasi-moral burden of choice: whom to invite, whom not to, whom we could get away with offending, who was centrally important to our lives—all that exasperating stuff had to be faced, and neither of us felt up to it. But there was a solution. It was Barcelona. Doris didn't have strong feelings about Barcelona—not yet—but I most emphatically did. I had been going there at intervals, to work and to disport myself, for more than thirty years. I had written a biography of the city, some ten years before: not a travel guide, nor really a formal history, but something like an attempt to evoke the genius loci of this great queen city of Catalunya, so little known even to educated foreigners then—and to tell the story of its development through its formidably rich deposit of buildings and artworks, and to show (necessarily in a small compass) what vitality could reside in "provincial" cultures, a project that had its natural appeal to a writer from another "provincial" place, Australia.

I don't think I have enjoyed writing any book as much as *Barcelona*. Years of research went into it, and long deep friendships were forged in the process. I also learned to read, if not fluently to speak, Catalan, and got some insight into the marvelous and rich literature that has been produced in it: a literature which has never been properly translated into English, because the effort of doing so for the small returns it would reap would break any publisher's back these days. Writing the book necessarily brought me close to the people who ran the city government, and to three consecutive mayors: Narcis Serra first, and then Pasqual Maragall (descendant of one of the cardinal *modernista* poets of Barcelona, Joan Maragall, 1860-1911), and finally his successor at the Ajuntament or Town Hall, Joan Clos. And then, as the right hand of all three successively, there was my beloved friend Margarita Obiols, the cultural minister of the socialist party of Barcelona who had watched over me through two failed marriages and was determined to see the third, which would also be the last, take place and stick together. And so—to make short work of what proved to be a diplomatic near-marathon, its complexities arising from the somewhat labyrinthine Spanish laws governing what *forasters* or non-Spaniards must do, not do, declare, and if necessary conceal in order to get married in Spain (for marrying there in the twenty-first century sometimes feels, for the non-Spaniard, as difficult as divorcing in the long-gone days of Franco)—Joan Clos and Margarita announced the glad news that we had been cleared to be married, and in Barcelona. Not only in Barcelona, but in the Town Hall, originally known as the Casa de la Ciutat ("house of the city"), and by Joan, in his capacity as *alcalde.* And not only by him

The Saló de Cent inside the Ajuntament

and in the Ajuntament, but in its most splendid and history-laden ceremonial room, the Saló de Cent (Hall of the Council of One Hundred).

The Saló de Cent housed the governing body of the city of Barcelona, which had developed out of an order by that great city-shaping king of the thirteenth century, Jaume I, who created a committee of twenty high-ranking citizens, known as peers or *probi homines* (in Catalan, *prohoms*) who would advise on city management. The group had among other abilities the power to convene general meetings of citizens, an important step on the much disputed road toward democracy as we understand it now. By 1274 a system emerged from this that, in essence, would govern Barcelona until it was erased by the Bourbons in Madrid in the early eighteenth century. A committee of seven people, made up of five *consellers,* the mayor, and the chief magistrate, picked a council of about a hundred representative citizens. They were drawn from all walks of life, cobblers and bakers as well as bankers and the upper mercantile orders. Although there were more of the latter, the vote of a tailor or a cooper had more or less the same weight as that of an international textile trader on the Consell de Cent. To some Catalans this seemed highly inconsistent: One might as well, complained a fifteenth-century political scribe named Jaume Safont, put *cabrós* (a ferociously insulting term, meaning literally "he-goats") on the committee as men of "vile condition." To a modern eye, of course, such a policy was the seedling of an egalitarian democracy, long before so radical an idea was launched in any other European state. The Consell de Cent was by a long way the oldest proto-democratic body in Europe. It enshrined the principle that, in a good and well-shaped society, things should happen by contract based on mutual regard rather than by divine right. The most famous political dictum of early Catalunya was uttered there—the unique oath of allegiance sworn by Catalans and Aragonese to the Spanish monarch in Madrid. "We, who are as good as you, swear to you, who are no better than us, to accept you as our king and sovereign lord, provided you observe all our liberties and laws—but if not, not."

This seemed then, and still does, a perfectly fair and admirable template for marriage as well. It would be an honor to be married in a room associated with such ideals, particularly since neither of us was a practicing Christian (one lapsed Catholic, one lapsed Episcopalian, one an atheist, the other an agnostic, both fond of ceremony but both churchgoers mainly for the sake of the architecture). Even today, when one thinks of monarchy as a decorative and essentially harmless fossil, those words from the Consell de Cent have the sharp and thrilling ring of political truth: They evoke a people who have no doubt about themselves and their identity *as* a people.

And what is more, a people who are not necessarily big respecters of other peoples' personages. Catalans had a traditional knack for putting kingship in perspective. On the facade of the Ajuntament there is a statue of a fifteenth-century merchant named Joan Fiveller. His effigy was put there in the 1850s instead of a figure of Hercules, as an emblem of civic strength. Why? Because at one point in his service as conseller to the city, the Castilian king of Catalunya and Aragon came on a state visit to Barcelona, with his retinue, which was of course large. And Fiveller endeared himself to the Catalans by insisting that the king and his traveling court should pay taxes on the *baccala,* the salt cod, they consumed. In doing so, he became an uncanonized patron saint of a tendency in Catalan political life which no authority has ever been able to extinguish—a sort of collectivist populism which expresses itself in citizens' associations and strikes. This demand was entirely a symbolic gesture— it's unlikely that the royal retinue could have been so big that its consumption of tax-free salt cod would have put very much of a strain on Barcelona's fiscus—but the point, it was felt, ought and had to be made. It applied to more serious expenditures, too. Thus in 1878, a gas strike left the city in darkness for a year because the Barcelonans balked at paying what they considered an exploitive municipal tax. Thus in 1951, they joined together to challenge the Franco regime with a tram strike, which paralyzed the city for weeks but indubitably got results. The whole historical tendency of Barcelonans has been to show themselves, not as mere spectators of the comings and goings of power, but as participants in it. They have always wanted something more, much more in fact, than mere "transparency."

The Saló de Cent was designed around 1360 by the architect Pere (Peter) Llobet and inaugurated in 1373. Badly damaged by bombardment in 1842 during a workers' uprising, it was rebuilt in the 1880s by the patriot architect Lluís Domènech i Montaner, a great figure who came within a split hair of being as remarkable, if more conservative, an architect as Antoni Gaudí. (Gaudí also entered the competition for the job of designing a new Saló de Cent, but his design got nowhere and since its drawings have long since been lost we have no idea what it may have looked like.) Some neo-Gothic decor was added in 1914, but it is still one of the noblest spaces in Spain. It also radiates ceremonial richness, not least because the upper half of its walls are hung in broad stripes of contrasting red and gold silk—a heraldic design based on and evoking the *quatres barres* (four stripes) of the Catalan flag. How did they get on the flag? Supposedly, as the finger marks of Charlemagne's son, Louis El Piados (the Pious), who created an armorial design for Wilfred the Hairy by dabbling his four royal digits in the wounded warrior's blood and scraping them down the shield— a sort of minimalist claw mark that has endured as Catalunya's sign for a thousand years. But the story has a catch: Wilfred the Hairy was born around A.D. 840 and died in about 897. Louis the Pious' corresponding dates were 778 and 840, which, if strictly insisted on, can only mean that he drew the four red bars in Wilfred's blood nearly half a century after his own death. This is a mystery whose solution lies beyond the historian's own fingers.

The December evening on which we were scheduled to be married was bright and cold and—unusually for Barcelona—dusted with snow. Whiteness clung to every stringcourse and crocket of the Cathedral's facade. It crunched underfoot. This early snowfall was seen by our Catalan friends as an omen, though exactly of what—beyond a generalized kind of happiness—no two of them seemed quite to agree. It rarely snows in Barcelona before Christmas. It hadn't done so in more than fifteen years—so this had to be an exceptional date. And it certainly felt like one. I have not forgotten, and never will, looking down from an embrasure of the Casa de la Ciutat at the cold medieval stone staircase and seeing Doris walking so gracefully up its shallow steps, unaware (I think) that I was watching her, slender in her white-and-pale-blue wedding dress, the sparse flakes of snow falling negligently, in slow motion, past her shoulders and seeming to rhyme with her pale and gleaming hair. Had I ever been so happy at a wedding before? No, I had not. I still can't imagine how one could be. The mayor, Joan Clos, hitched us in Catalan and very slightly awkward English. We answered in awkward Catalan: "*Si, vull*—Yes, I want to." Doris's younger son, Fielder, produced the rings with perfect aplomb, not missing a beat. My fear that he might drop one of them, and that we would see it rolling into a crack between the old paving stones of the Saló de Cent, was quite unfounded. A string quartet played, sweetly and ceremoniously. And then it was down the stairs, into various cars, and off south and uphill to Esplugües de Llobregat, to the house of the best man who was, inevitably, the sculptor Xavier Corberó, who had begun my love affair with Barcelona and changed my life so many years ago by introducing me to *la gran encisera,* the great enchantress, as the nineteenth-century Catalan poet Joan Maragall called his native city.

The wedding dinner was held in Xavier's masia. His caterers had set up eight tables. To reach them you had to walk across a threshold strewn with aromatic branches of wild rosemary, which brings fortune and length to the marriage. We were given, first, a thick soup of white beans flecked with black grains of pureed truffle, and surmounted by a solid slice of duck foie gras. (This was so delicious that both my teenage stepsons, Garrett and Fielder, clamored for second and then third ladlefuls of it.) Then came a piece of roast *lubina* or sea bass, reticently perfumed with thyme. Then roast capon, garnished with a variety of wild mushrooms from the Catalan hill forests: *rovellons, ous de reig,* and the black sinister-sounding *trompetes de mort,* death trumpets. Finally, the wedding cake, four tiers of it, white, creamy, and unctuous, surmounted by a marzipan Doris and a marzipan Bob, in wedding attire, holding hands. We took a carving knife, which looked almost as impressive as the blade of Wilfred the Hairy, and plunged it right in, four hands on its hilt. Neither of my previous weddings had featured a cake with a tiny bride and groom, and I was enchanted. Neither of us quite broke down and cried, although I know that I was within a few millimeters of doing so.

I thought about a lot of things during that party, though with increasing muzziness as the evening lengthened. Mainly about Doris, about happiness, and about loyalty: to her, and to old friends like Corberó, who probably knows me better than any living man, including my own relatives, just as my relations with Barcelona are so much closer and more pleasurable than with anywhere south of the Equator.

Some provincials—and there is one in most Australian hearts, including mine—struggle to throw off the stigma of their provincialism by relating chiefly, or in some cases only, to the huge cultural centers: New York, Paris, London. And in fact I have lived and worked longer in New York (thirty-three years) than in Australia (which I left at twenty-six). But I have never lost my tropism for the big small town that feels like home. Hence, my feelings about Barcelona.

Once, when I thought about becoming a citizen of some country other than Australia, I used to consider America—never England, of course, for that would have felt like a colonial capitulation, a craven wriggle backward into a womb that was not likely to be very welcoming. But then it was borne in on me that to be an American, even an adoptive one, was automatically and by definition to be a colonialist, and to become one by law was only to be a secondhand, adoptive colonialist. America by now was as imperial as England had been fifty years before my birth. Was I ever going to feel excited if my prospective fellow citizens colonized the moon, or visited Mars, or carried out the scientific, ideological, or cultural schemes that seemed to be boiling away in the scary limbic forebrains of America's rulers—a bunch of strangers who, in George W. Bush's phrase, already viewed my native country as their "sheriff" in the Pacific? No way, Hozay. This species of derivative grandeur was soggy, boring stuff. If you are going to change your citizenship, better to fly or flounder under the flag of a place that once had an enormous empire but now has none; that doesn't pretend (or, as Americans like to say, "aspire") to world moral leadership; that treats "inspiring" public discourse with a certain reticence and skepticism. How about being Catalan for a change? Well, I guess we shall see.

Back in the 1960s it was easier to imagine being dead than being over sixty and, as duly confessed, I had no more idea of Barcelona than I did of Atlantis. What little I knew of the city was that three decades before, in the name of the Spanish Republic, it had resisted General Franco (1892-1975) and paid a heavy, bitter price for it; that George Orwell, one of my literary heroes, had written a book about it called *Homage to Catalonia;* that in that book he had got most things right, but had been spectacularly wrong in dissing the admittedly very peculiar Antoni Gaudí, claimed by the French surrealists, who had designed that enormous penitential church seemingly made of melted candle wax and chicken guts.

If my knowledge of Barcelona some forty years ago was lamentably slight, so was that of most Europeans and Americans. Not just slight—embarrassingly so. So embarrassing that we weren't even embarrassed by it. The 1,500 years of the city's existence had produced only five names that came readily to mind. There was Gaudí, of course, and the century's greatest cellist, Pau Casals. There were the painters Salvador Dalí, Joan

Miró, and Pablo Picasso, who though he was actually born in Málaga and spent nearly all his long working life in France had become a sort of honorary Catalan, having attended art school there and used the city as his point of departure for Paris. Of other Catalan artists who were older than Picasso, and were at the time very much his superiors—that superbly fluent and piercing draftsman Ramón Casas comes to mind, among others—we were quite ignorant. We had heard about Gaudí but we got him entirely wrong, because we knew little or nothing about his deeply Catalan roots, his obsession with craft culture, and his deeply right-wing piety. We thought he was some kind of proto-surrealist weirdo, which trivializes his achievement. We simply had no idea where to put him, and this was largely due to the fact that, although he was so manifestly a radical artist, we were too blinded by the rhetoric of the 1960s to imagine a radicalism that was both right wing and intensely fruitful.

On the other hand, we probably wouldn't have recognized the name of an almost equally great architect, Lluís Domènech i Montaner, or even been able to pronounce that of Josep Puig i Cadafalch (1867-1957), one of the most erudite and sophisticated designers ever to work in Europe. For the record, Puig, which means "peak," is pronounced pooch, and this gave rise to a silly piece of doggerel, supposedly by a friend of that great Majorcan expatriate Robert Graves, which began:

> *How I would love to climb the Puig,*
> *And watch the peasants huigy-cuig:*
> *Beneath the plane-trees I would muig,*
> *Upon the benches we would smuig …*

We had no idea of how that singular piece of nineteenth-century utopian town planning, the Eixample or "enlargement" of Barcelona into a grid of equal squares that surrounds the original, medieval city, came into its existence, or who its designer, Ildefons Cerdà, was. The few guides to Catalan architecture in print back in the 1960s were unreliable and never in English. There was practically nothing on Catalan painting, though the world's greatest surviving body of Romanesque frescoes, salvaged from decaying churches in the Ampurdan and the Pyrenees, was (and is) right there in the Museu d'Art de Catalunya up on Montjuïc. No foreign visitor, except a few specialists who knew Catalan, could possibly get acquainted with the great writers and poets of Barcelona's past, from Ramón Llull and Ausiàs March in the Middle Ages to Jacint Verdaguer and Joan Maragall in the nineteenth century. Some of Barcelona's finest writers will never be translated because their work is either too voluminous (there are, for instance, more than thirty volumes of Josep Pla's essays and biographical sketches) or too local, or both.

Back in the 60s and 70s, Xavier Corberó and his friends—writers, artists, architects, economists, fledgling politicians—hoped to change this. What did they want? They imagined Barcelona becoming, as it had been in the past, a center of Mediterranean culture. Not *the* center: that, in the twentieth century, would have been impossible, and undesirable anyway. Centralism was exactly what Catalans had struggled against for the past several centuries—it connoted the tyrannous hand of Francoism and the dictator's insistence that Catalunya, which had always disliked and resisted him, was a mere province of Madrid and its language, Catalan, a mere dialect of Castilian Spanish. They saw his rule as only the last in a long series of efforts by Habsburg and Bourbon monarchs, from the seventeenth century onward, to deprive Catalunya of its *autodeterminació,* its self-government. They wanted to help Barcelona recapture some of the luster it had half a century before their birth, back in the 1880s. That would have to be a tall order, since this period, known to Catalans as their *Renaixenca* or rebirth into *modernisme,* which didn't exactly mean modernism as understood a century later, was forgotten by almost everyone in 1966, except the Catalans themselves—and imperfectly remembered by them. Its monuments and buildings were all around Barcelona but there was surprisingly little unanimity of opinion about what they meant.

None of these young people were Communists though a few were Marxists. Their general freedom from ideological constraint was one of those qualities which, thirty years later, helped to save Barcelona as a city and as a culture: a firm belief in the social responsibility of government, coupled with an equally strong conviction that cultures start with the individual and are not made on ideological command. This was the generation of Catalans, little known at the time—as next generations always are—that was going to change the city, and I had the enormous good luck to have them, along with Xavier, as my guides. I felt especially receptive to them because by the late 1960s I was getting fed up the back teeth with the imperial pretensions of American modernism; the idea, suffocating in its application even though once fairly liberating in its earlier assertion, that New York was now the center of everything worth having in the arts of painting and sculpture, not to mention the practice of art criticism, and that nothing counted if not ratified there. Maybe this was true and maybe not, but it wasn't something you could just assume, particularly if you were an Australian living in Europe. There had to be more to life, I thought, than all those hectares of lyric acrylic on unprimed duck; it might just be that Jackson Pollock, God rest his gifted, drunken soul, was not a creator of the same order as Winslow Homer or Marsden Hartley; and what was so incontrovertible about Clem Greenberg anyway, let alone the flat dry prose of his imitators? I can't say I was altogether unbiased. I know my Catalan friends weren't. They were the patriots, of a country other than Spain. They were Spanish *and* Catalan, and it is true beyond doubt that Spaniards and especially Catalans tend to put their homeland first in their affections.

Sometimes this loyalty attains a certain craziness for which one must learn to make allowances. Once, several years ago, I was having lunch with the Catalan architect Oriol Bohigas before, as I planned, catching the air shuttle to Madrid. It was late in the afternoon—we hadn't sat down to eat until 2:00, and to my horror when I looked at my watch it was already just shy of 4:00 and we weren't yet through our sausage and beans, the *butifarra amb monguetes,* which is one of the classic peasant dishes of Catalunya. Stricken, I told Oriol that I had miscalculated badly.

"Not possible. Where are you heading for?"

"Madrid."

"*Madrid?*"

"Yes, Madrid."

"But in Madrid," said Oriol with an air of puzzled finality, "in Madrid there is *nothing.*" He swallowed a glass of excellent rioja and beamed at me.

"Well, there's the Prado," I rejoined feebly.

"Oh well, the Prado," said Oriol with the air of a man who extends a trivial concession to a friend who, come down to it, doesn't know too much. "Yes, there is the Prado. Of course. But I know you have been to it before, so what's the hurry?"

One main reason why Barcelona seemed hard to penetrate—apart from the unfamiliarity of its language, Catalan—was that it had decayed so badly since the loss of the civil war. Spain's dictator, Franco, hated the place and wanted revenge on it for opposing him. He had been in the saddle so long that most Catalans did not remember a world without him. After him, Spain had to be reinvented, a daunting if exhilarating prospect. The father of one of my best friends there had put away, years before, a magnum of fine champagne (Krug, I think). When Franco died he was going to open it, but not before. Franco's death was heralded by a fusillade of popping corks all over Barcelona, but not my friend's; it had been sitting in the fridge so long that it had gone flat. So, in a sense, had the city itself. *Barcelona grisa,* gray Barcelona, was how people referred to it, looking back on the years of Franco and his much despised Falangist mayor, Josep Maria de Porcioles i Colomer, who ran the most intellectually inert and historically oblivious city government of the twentieth century. Barcelona had turned into a sort of sleeping princess, neglected, and ignored. It was one enormous ashtray, covered in a mantle of grime and grit. The buildings that should have made it famous were suffocating and in decay. Even its great Christian monuments, like the Cathedral, had repulsive administrative-modern office blocks jammed next to them, an ugly modernism that signified contempt and seemed to mock the ostentatious piety of Franco's regime. Things were done to the nineteenth-century architectural masterpieces of Barcelona—Gaudí's Casa Milà, Domènech i Montaner's Casa Lle, Morera and his Palau de la Música Catalana—that would never have been allowed to happen to buildings from the medieval era, because although the earlier ones were rightly seen as historically precious, the later ones were wrongly thought of as old-fashioned or grotesque. (It should, in fairness, be added that Franco's appalling or merely sluggish and greedy lieutenants were not shy about applying the wrecker's ball to medieval buildings, secular ones, in other Spanish cities.)

And, of course, it wasn't only the Falangists who thought art nouveau was disposable rubbish. Here is

George Orwell, in *Homage to Catalonia,* on Gaudí's Sagrada Família: "one of the most hideous buildings in the world ... I think the anarchists showed bad taste in not blowing it up when they had the chance." At least he gave the old man a mention, as did Evelyn Waugh, who for some inscrutable reason decided that another Gaudí building, the Casa Batlló on Passeig de Gràcia, was the Turkish Consulate. Sir Nikolaus Pevsner didn't even include Gaudí in his canonical *Pioneers of Modern Design.*

The Barcelona we value so much today had been punitively raped and degraded by business, by the unsupervised and opportunistic greed of developers, who set to work on its fabric not like artists or surgeons, but like amnesiac butchers who were also good family men. Was this the result of deliberately planned policy? The answer has to be No, *but.* No, *but* decay is a most powerful force, and amnesia too. No, *but* it's hard not to see in Barcelona's deterioration during the Porcioles years (1957-1973) the unfolding of a vengeful desire for entropy. Barcelona had resisted the caudillo. Bad idea. There would be money for cement works outside the city, because the businessmen who owned them were Franco supporters. But there was not going to be money to restore the great symbolic works of Catalanist architecture, like the Palau de la Música Catalana, because these, like the best of the city's culture, were opposed to

the very spirit of Madrid centralism, of rule from outside Barcelona itself.

BARCELONA WAS SHAPED, AND ITS DESTINY DETERMINED,
by the fact that it began as a port and has been one ever
since. Exactly when this birth occurred cannot now be
fixed. At one point, there was a thin speckle of Bronze
Age settlement by the sea there, extending up the sea-
ward flank of what is now Montjuïc, the mountain
which rears up to your right as you look out to sea from
the waterfront. The people who inhabited it were known
as the Laietani; they were, as far as anyone knows, indige-
nous; they were one of the various branches the Celtic
tribesmen who, in prehistoric times, had come down
across the Pyrenees to the coastal plains of what is now
Catalunya and interbred with the resident Iberians,
themselves the product and residue of earlier invasions
from North Africa. Practically nothing is known about
the Laietani. They did not have a written language
(again, as far as anyone knows), which suggests that they
did not trade except among themselves. One of the principal streets of modern Barcelona is known as the Via
Laietana, and was so christened when an urban renewal

scheme demanded a straight cut from hillside to water-front; but there isn't a smidgen of evidence that its track, when pushed through in 1908, had anything to do with the elusive Laietani, and little trace of them—no arti-facts, let alone buildings—was found in the excavations. A small fossil of their presence may have been (not cer-tainly, only possibly) the name Barcino, which supposedly meant "welcoming port." Current fashions in history tend to favor the underdog, but even allowing for that the Laietani would seem to have achieved little, made less, and vanished almost without a trace under the heel of the Romans, who colonized this part of the Spanish coast as a base from which to run their war against the Carthaginians in 210 B.C. Even so, the future Barcelona did not become a significant colony—or not right away. That honor belonged to Tarraco (the future Tarragona), conquered in 210 B.C. by the ferocious young general Scipio Africanus Major, who marched south the next year and utterly destroyed the Punic base of Carthago Nova. Tarraco was rich. So was Carthago Nova, whose silver mines alone brought in twenty-five thousand drachmas a day. These were colonial possessions worth having. Not so the future Barcelona, which produced little but fish, and a once much esteemed breed of local oyster—long since, alas, rendered extinct by the industrial pollution of the harbor water.

But when the Romans conquered a place, they took it over completely and re-formed it in their image. So it was with the little settlement that straggled up the slope of Montjuïc—a name, incidentally, that may (but again, not certainly) derive from Mons Iovis, the "hill of Jupiter." The problem with Montjuïc was its lack of water. But two streams ran down from the plain to the beach, and it made sense to relocate the town (if it were to grow) between them, on a small, and today barely perceptible, eminence named Mont Taber. These framed the new city, which was hardly more than a village. It covered about thirty acres and was shaped liked a fat boot heel. Roughly at its center was the forum, which lies beneath what is still the administrative core of Barcelona—the Plaça Sant Jaume, between the Ajuntament, the seat of city government, and the Palau de la Generalitat, which houses the state government of Catalunya. In essence it was a Roman military camp, but one defined and outlined by thick masonry brick and cement walls. But small and rather ad hoc though Barcino (as it was named) might be, it still signified Rome, the greatest power on Earth, and consequently the cult of the Roman emperor and the Roman gods. Hence its temple dedicated to the Emperor Augustus, of which a few remains survive in the form of three Corinthian columns in the basement of a house at No. 10, Carrer del

Paradis, just off Plaça Sant Jaume. They don't look like much. But on the other hand, none of the Roman relics of Barcelona do, except perhaps for a few parts of the old city wall, massive and obdurate and much built into by later construction. The lower levels of Barcelona are not a Pompeii. If you expected the interest of this ancient city to reside in its most ancient parts, you would be sorely disappointed.

No sooner had Roman Barcelona begun to attain a respectable size than the decay and contraction of the Spanish part of the Roman Empire itself began to work against it, pulling it back to inconsequence and provinciality. In a series of maneuvers and takeovers too complicated to recite here, a series of barbarian invasions from Germany came down across the Pyrenees, starting around A.D. 409: Vandals, Suevians, Alani, and finally a force of (perhaps) 250,000 Visigoths, commanded by their king, Ataulf. The Visigoths have had an unjust press, denounced as destroyers and brutes. But quite a lot had rubbed off on them in the few years since they devastated Greece and sacked Rome. In fact, they had become enthusiastic churchbuilders and in the late sixth century one of their kings, Reccared, imposed Catholicism over Arianism as the official state religion in northern Spain. (So much for a famously silly claim by one American neo-con writer in the 1980s, that the universities and higher institutions of learning in his country were being taken over by "Visigoths in tweed." If only, one can hear more informed neo-cons groaning.)

Only fragments—and fragments of fragments, at that—survive to mark the Visigoths' Christian presence in Barcelona. The sculptures of evangelists, a lion (Mark), an angel (Matthew), an eagle (John), and the hand of God, which are built into the facade of tiny Sant Pau del Camp, the oldest church in the city, were salvaged and recycled from what was probably a Visigothic chapel on the site. But apart from that, virtually nothing of Visigothic Barcelona remains. What is even more surprising is that no buildings survive that were erected by the great unifier of the Catalan Dark Ages in the middle of the ninth century, and who was mythologized by Catalans for a thousand years after his death as the founder of Catalunya's national independence. This man was known as Guifré el Pelos—Wilfred the Hairy.

Wilfred established his rule of Catalunya by defeating a Frankish overlord, while presiding over the expulsion from Barcelona of the Saracens, who had managed to conquer the city—the next-to-last time any Arabs would get into Barcelona. Despite the nearly intact Roman walls of the little city, the *sarrains*—who had become a big inconvenience to trade, a wasp's nest of

Moorish freebooters—were thrown out, or so the story goes, by an alliance between Wilfred the Hairy and Charlemagne's son, Louis the Pious, in 801. (Their respective dates, as we have already seen, make this impossible, but never mind. In terms of heraldry, politics, and myth, the idea of Catalan independence begins with him.)

Wilfred the Hairy, having consolidated his hold on northern Catalunya, became an enthusiastic supporter of monasteries and churches, thereby getting the priestly scribes on his side and ensuring himself an excellent press. He endowed almost all the earliest church foundations of Catalunya: Santa Maria de Formiguera (873), Santa Maria de la Grassa (878), Santa Maria de Ripoll (888), and Sant Pere de Ripoll (890) among them. He built himself a palace in Barcelona, of which nothing remains. He endowed churches there, which have also vanished. If Barcelona is devoid of Carolingian buildings, it is not because the Moors, led by the vizier of Córdoba, briefly retook it in 985, but because of early Catalan "developers" who flattened them during Barcelona's first building boom in the twelfth to fourteenth centuries. Early churches in the north, in the towns at the foot of the Pyrenees, which had been established by Wilfred, survived perfectly well and one of them, Santa Maria de Ripoll, is still sometimes called the *bressol de Catalunya* (cradle of Catalunya) and features a magnificent though timeworn alabaster portal, the finest Romanesque sculptural complex in all of Spain.

Under the line of count-kings that began with Wilfred the Hairy, the territory of Catalunya expanded steadily. Its crucial political event, which came in the twelfth century, was the marriage of the Catalan count-king Ramón Berenguer IV to Petronella, the queen of neighboring Aragon. This fused Catalunya and Aragon into a large power bloc, formidable enough to keep at bay any incursion from Castile and to fend off the centralist ambitions of the kings in Madrid. Moreover, since their military forces combined, the union of Catalunya and Aragon created a Catalan empire in the Mediterranean. Beginning with Jaume I, who amply deserved his sobriquet El Conqueridor, the Conqueror, the kingdom of Aragon and Catalunya had an empire by the beginning of the fourteenth century.

The tangible symbol of this was the Llotja, the "lodge"—in effect, the first stock exchange in Europe or anywhere else. The Llotja, in its original Gothic form, was constructed in the fourteenth century, as part of the first of the three largest building booms in Catalan history. The first of these booms, which produced the

Llotja and a large amount of the *casc antic* or medieval city besides, was set going by a singular and obsessive monarch, Pere III, known as El Ceremonios, who ruled Barcelona for much of the fourteenth century.

The second took place in the last quarter of the nine-teenth century, and it gave us that stupendous and visionary city plan, the first of the grid cities, the ances-tor of New York: the Eixample, conceived by Ildefons Cerdà, the New Barcelona that broke out of the con-stricting *muralles* and enabled the city to grow beyond its imposed medieval limits.

And the third building boom was the restoration and refiguring of Barcelona in the years leading up to and then beyond the Olympics of 1992, set in motion by the mayor Pasqual Maragall.

Catalan building booms tend to have something in common. They defy common sense. This was spectac-ularly true of what happened under the rule of Peter the Ceremonious. He was a proud man with a quick and dangerous temper. He liked luxury and elaborate protocol and he wanted his city to testify to what he perceived as the glories of his own singular character. He set this ambition forth in a poem, for he was a poet, too—maybe not a great one like Ausiàs March, but not a bad one for a ruler. In its original medieval Catalan it runs:

Lo loch me par sia pus degut
noble ciutat, o vila gross'e gran,
o.ls enaemichs valentment garreian
tenent al puny lança e'l brac escut,
o'n esglesia, on devotate sia,
e si u fa'xi, no sera ja repres
per cavallers ...

Which in modern translation means, more or less:

The worthiest of places, so I think
is a noble city, or a great fine town
or to be bravely fighting enemies
with lance in hand, or shield upon one's arm
or at one's devotions in a church
and if I do this, then I will not be scorned
by noble knights ...

He couldn't have been plainer about this. Cities exist to promote the glory of their inhabitants, their citizens, and, in particular, their rulers. If they don't or can't do this, they are not fit to be called cities; they are merely villages, large or small. The status of a city can be gauged from the glory of its institutions. Some of these are religious, of course, but others are civil. And since there was no city in the

Mediterranean world more religiously devoted to money than Barcelona, Catalan commerce had to have its own cathedral. Clearly, what Peter the Ceremonious and his Catalan contemporaries wanted was to build, on the edge of the sea which was the source of their wealth, a kind of medieval World Trade Center—though one which could not be destroyed by the Arabs, who were still in command of most of Spain south of the Ebro.

They wanted to build much more, and they did. To make sure the *moros* would not get in, they remade the city walls. They built a huge wall that started on the sea, just south of the Drassanes, the earlier medieval shipyards, and enclosed the whole area that now lies between the Ramblas and the Paral-lel. It enclosed the *horts i vinyets,* the market gardens on which Barcelona's emergency food supply depended. It was a giant garden fence. That was a strategic necessity. But what was not so plausible were the efforts and money they expended on a whole range of buildings we now see as the essence of medieval Barcelona. The Casa de la Ciutat; the Saló del Tinell with its stupendous arches—those semicircular rainbows of stone; Santa Maria del Mar; much of the Cathedral; and, of course, the Llotja. Were these and other masterpieces of the Barri Gòtic (Old City) raised in a time of peace and prosperity?

Absolutely not. In 1333 the Catalan wheat crop failed and about ten thousand people, a quarter of the city's population, starved to death. Barcelona was teetering on the edge of bankruptcy. That was what gave the background to this great building its bizarre and manic quality. Think about New York for a moment. The greatest city in the world was traumatized almost to the point of paralysis by a terrorist attack which killed fewer than three thousand people, out of a population of eight million. Less than 0.1 percent. But here was a fourteenth-century city which in one year lost about 25 percent of its population, and still built continuously, with an unquenchable belief in the future—even though it was at the same time being attacked by other assorted acts of God as well.

Plague, for instance. Because Barcelona was a great sea-trading city, it was unusually and directly vulnerable to the plague, whose germs, *Yersina pestis,* came in the saliva of lice, which rode on the skin of rats, which crossed the Mediterranean in the holds of ships. The city's economy was just beginning to recover from the catastrophes of the 1330s when plague struck in 1348. Majorca was the first part of Europe to get it, and then Catalunya. Eighty percent of the population of the Balearic Islands died. In Barcelona government was nearly wiped out: Four out of the five consellers died, for instance. The result of the Black Death, here as elsewhere, was social chaos. Those with a millenarian view announced that the Last Judgment and the Final Days were coming. Many blamed it on the Jews, and every Catalan knew someone who knew someone else who had seen Jews throwing corpses in Christian wells. So along with the epidemics and renewed cycles of famine there were lynch mobs and pogroms. If you wanted a textbook example of how medieval states and polities could come apart and collapse, you could not find a better one than Barcelona at the time that the Llotja was being built, under the reign of Peter the Ceremonious. Truly, the living envied the dead, and everyone feared the hand of God was against them. And yet they continued to build, in the face of disasters that none of them understood.

They found refuge and solace in religion, so perhaps it is not a mystery that the calamitous fourteenth century was the great period of Catalan church building. But the Catalans, then as now, took great pride in their mercantile hardheadedness and they had already elevated business to a kind of state religion, which had the advantage of letting bankers and wholesalers in baccala feel like the gods, heroes, and saints they always knew they were. And that was why they built La Llotja del Mar, right at the height of the plague, between 1380 and 1392.

The Llotja

A *llotja* is a business exchange. Most actively trading cities in the old *paisos Catalanes* in southern France and northeastern Spain had such lodges—Perpignan, Aix, Palma, and so on. But the llotjas of Palma and Barcelona were by far the grandest and most permanent of them.

This reflected Barcelona's preeminence as a trading city, at a time when Madrid was hardly more than a cluster of mud huts beside the Manzanares River, and no idea of a Spanish empire run from it had yet been conceived. The count-kings of Catalunya had consulates in no fewer than 126 places across the Mediterranean. Their mercantile empire stretched from Venice to Beirut, from Málaga to Constantinople, from Famagusta to Tripoli, from Montpellier to Cairo. No other country had such a network. They traded everywhere and with everybody. To the Levant they exported woolen cloth and sheepskins, dried fruit, olive oil, and iron. In return they got pepper, incense, cinnamon, and thousands on thousands of slaves. To the Balearic Islands, Sardinia, Naples, and Sicily, which made up the Catalan empire in the fourteenth century, they exported cloth, leather goods, saffron, and arms; they brought back cotton, wheat, baccala, and more slaves. They traded in textiles with Flanders and in everything from dried figs to nuts and miles of cloth with the cities of the Barbary Coast of North Africa. This trade was mainly carried on by Catalan Jews, who would be furiously persecuted by stupid Spanish Christians in the fifteenth century but at the time the Llotja was being built in the fourteenth were not only tolerated but encouraged by the pragmatic Catalans, for the simple reason that a Jew could set up as a trading agent in Muslim cities from which Christians were excluded.

No medieval culture, then, was as forthright in its commitment to the virtues of business as that of fourteenth-century Catalunya. And none would be until the English in the nineteenth century, whose dithyrambs in praise of money and the middle class remind one so strongly of the Catalans. Only one thing was better than a merchant, and that was two merchants. In the 1380s a former Franciscan theologian, Francesc de Eiximenis, published a four-volume work of 2,500 chapters called *Regiment de la Cosa Publica,* in which he argued that the only protection citizens had against warlords and tyrants was a strong, dominant middle class. The bourgeois, full of *seny* (common sense) and public spirit, were virtue itself. They should be a protected species. "Merchants," Eiximenis declared, "should be favored above all other lay people in the world ... they are the life of the people, the treasure of public interest, the food of the poor, the arm of all good commerce.... Without merchants, societies fall apart, princes become tyrants, the young are lost and the poor weep.... Only merchants are big givers and great fathers and brothers of the common good."

The relation between cash, power, and sanctity was much more briefly expressed by a Majorcan poet named Anselm Turmeda, who at the end of the fourteenth century urged his readers,

> *Diners, doncs, vulles aplegar.*
> *Si els pots haver no els lleixs anar:*
> *Si molts n'hauras poràs tornar*
> *papa de Roma.*

So you must get money!
If you get it, don't let it go!
If you get a lot, then you can be
The Pope of Rome!

So as architecture, the Llotja had a definite mission. It was to affirm the values of the middle class and impress everyone—including, of course, its own members—with their permanent importance. In this sense it was a true cathedral of commerce. There had been an earlier Llotja. But it was small, hardly more than a stone pavilion set back a little from the beach, though designed by a distinguished architect—Pere Llobet, best known today for designing the Saló de Cent in the Ajuntament. It was destroyed by flood tides in the 1350s, and this gave Peter the Ceremonious his opportunity to have it replaced on a much larger scale. The chosen architect was Pere Arbei, and it was the only substantial work he did in Barcelona. All that remains of it is one hall, but it is one of the world's greatest Gothic spaces and it tells us a lot about the essential nature of Catalan Gothic. That nature is wide, rather than tall. English and French fourteenth-century buildings were apt to release their energies, their architectural meaning, through the virtuoso display of their own height. Catalan architects preferred breadth to height:

Instead of soaring upward, a habit which the French thought transcendent but which the Catalans felt was somehow flimsy, their buildings spread, enclose, and remind you of their roots in the cave, the grotto; they speak of a sort of troglodytic piety. Width and length, not height, was what gave medieval Catalans a feeling of security and achievement. You see it in the churches, too: in Santa Maria del Pi, for instance, whose single nave is fifty-four feet wide, about a third of its length—an astonishing structural achievement in unsupported, unreinforced stonework, which usually can't carry big spans because of its weakness in tension. English and French Gothic architects reveled in dissolving the wall, turning it into stone lacework, depriving it of solid mass, and substituting glass instead. Not the Catalans of the fourteenth century, who like their Romanesque and Cistercian predecessors liked their buildings to look much stronger, heavier, and opaque.

The main hall of the Llotja, the so-called Sala de Contratacion or Contract Room, where most of the trading deals were hammered out, belongs to this family of structures. It is a big stone box whose roof is carried on three double bays of diaphragm arches. These six arches spring from four tall slender columns, elegantly quatrefoil in section. The arches are round—not pointed, as in northern Gothic—and the roof itself is not vaulted, but flat. It is made of massive beams, closely spaced and laid across the top of the diaphragms. In other words, it is very much the same structural system as the great Saló del Tinell, also designed by an architect working for Peter the Ceremonious, except that there the arches are not borne up on columns at all; they spring directly out of the floor, thus giving the hall the look of an enormous tunnel. Because of its columns, which are fluted and very slender, Pere Arbei's design is lighter and more soaring than this, but it is still nothing like French or English Gothic. You can see the structural system even more plainly from a gallery that runs around the wall of the Contract Room. It's a great interior, very forthright, very moving in its plainness. One of the greatest aspects of Catalan Gothic is its willingness to show you its bones, and that is what the Llotja was designed to do.

It was the basis and center, the meeting point of Catalan financial life. But though the greatness of the building remained, its usefulness did not, at least not indefinitely. The reason, basically, was simple. The old financial centrality of Barcelona was eroded; in effect, it was taken away by Madrid.

A succession of political events tore at the ancient independence of the kingdoms of Aragon and Catalunya. These culminated in 1714, with the conquest of Barcelona by a force of Spanish troops sent by the Bourbon king in Madrid, Felipe V (1683-1746), under the command of the bastard son of King James II, an English general also called the Duke of Berwick and afterward, among his many Spanish titles, El Duque de Liria. He had been sent to break the neck of Catalan resistance, and he did so. Its vestiges now lie in a common grave of the Catalan resisters next to Santa Maria del Mar, where the patriots slaughtered by Berwick's men after the city surrendered are buried.

Al fossar de les Moreres
no s'hi einterra cap traidor
Ffins perdent nostres banderes,
sera l'urna de l'honor.

In the Moreres graveyard,
no traitor is buried:
Even though we lost our flags
this will be the urn of honor.

The siege and conquest of Barcelona, and its reduction to a mere province of Madrid, a vassal state of a centralized Bourbon Spain, naturally had severe results for the Llotja and the work that was done in it. To begin with, the building was badly damaged in the bombardments of the siege—its columns were weakened and there was a fear of collapse. Politically, Barcelona lost much of its trading power and as a punishment for its treasonous hopes of independence from Madrid, it was forbidden to take part in the transatlantic trade with South America—which by now was far more profitable than medieval business relations with the Levant. Business with America would be reserved for Madrid and it would not flow through the Llotja. This did not last long. However, it became one of the most cherished parts of the mythology of Catalan separatism: the belief, still held by some Catalan ultraseparatists down to the present day—not that there are many left now—that the vengeful Bourbons wanted to crush, mangle, and annihilate all aspects of Catalan identity, starting with its language, and that a concerted campaign to impoverish the city was part of this. The villain of the piece, in popular imagination, was Felipe V, who was so hated by most Catalans that, not so long ago, when Barcelona school kids wanted to go to the *cagador* (toilet), they spoke of "going to visit Felipe." A good deal of this was the mythmaking of local patriotism. But it was true that the Bourbon conquest of Barcelona did close the Llotja down for a while; it was converted into a barracks for Felipe's troops, who had nowhere else to sleep.

However, it was Felipe's son Carlos III (1716-1788) who set Catalan business back on its feet again and made it possible not only to restore the Llotja but to greatly expand it and its influence. He did the first of these by lifting the ban on Barcelona's trade with the South American colonies—Mexico, Peru, Venezuela, Cuba, Puerto Rico, and the rest. From now on Catalan ships would be shuttling across the Atlantic, and Catalan venture capitalists would be founding impressive fortunes everywhere from Lima to Havana. To cope with the new scale of business, the Llotja had to be modernized and expanded. Its antiquated Gothic form would no longer do.

Carlos III was, by earlier standards, a moderately enlightened monarch. His tastes were neoclassic and he liked to see building on a grand scale, in the Italian manner. When he was the monarch of Naples, he had overseen the grandiose construction of the Palazzo di Caserta, and in Madrid he had brought in the Italian architect Filippo Juvarra to supervise the building of the enormous Palacio Real with its 1,200 rooms. Clearly, his glories as a patron of Catalan business were not going to be increased by merely restoring an old Gothic building that had been badly damaged by his father's armies. His administration, therefore, encouraged the Junta de Comerc to go ahead with what amounted to the construction of a new Llotja, in the style that the taste of his reign preferred, not a nostalgic

Gothic but what was considered the newest and best: an orderly, finely proportioned if rather heavy kind of neoclassicism, a shell which enclosed the old Gothic core and left no hint of its existence on the outside. Barcelona was not rich in neoclassic architects, but there was one who seemed to fit the requirements. Born in 1731, his name was Joan Soler i Faneca, and the new Llotja, for which he started drawing up plans in 1764, was his first major building in Barcelona. There would be two others, neither of the same importance: the Palau Sessa-Larrard, finished in 1778, and the Casa March de Reus, done in 1780.

All three are in the sober, conservative, and rather uninventive style that was de rigeur in later eighteenth-century Barcelona, but the best of them—indeed, the best neoclassic building in the city—was Soler's design for the Llotja. It has had a curious and hybrid past. It was finished in 1804 and for a while in the late nineteenth and early twentieth centuries half its top floor housed the main art school in Barcelona, *Escola de Bellas Artes* (School of Fine Arts). Picasso's father taught there, and young Pablo studied there in the late 1890s, as did Joan Miró and many lesser known nineteenth-century Catalan painters and sculptors. As a building it is balanced and elegant. Most of the decorative sculpture is mediocre, as sculpture tended to be in Barcelona, but there is one work of genuinely outstanding quality, a figure of the virtuous Lucrezia dying, having stabbed herself after her rape by the villainous Tarquin. It was finished in 1804 by the Catalan artist Damià Campeny, who had moved to Rome and worked there most of his life in a high neo-classic style derived from Antonio Canova.

Soler's design of the windows is plain, with very minimal detailing. The entrance courtyard is beautifully proportioned, and it contains the most memorable and interesting part of the building: the sweeping, double staircase, intensely sculptural, which undulates in a way that reminds me of Gaudí. In fact it may have had some influence on Gaudí, Barcelona's greatest architect. For it was Gaudí who helped to found a very influential society of artists called the Artistic Circle of St. Luke. It was ultraconservative, ultranationalist, and ultra, ultra Catholic, very much opposed to the kind of freethinking and ironic modernism that was practiced by Ramón Casas and Santiago Rusinyol in Els Quatre Gats café. Except for Gaudí and the sculptor Josep Llimona, none of its members went on to have a great effect on Catalan art, let alone Spanish art in general. But the interesting thing to me is that to go to the meetings the "Lukes" had in the art school, they had to go up that pierced and twisting staircase in the Llotja, and I don't think it's at all fanciful to see in its serpentine and almost liquid shapes the genesis of certain forms of Gaudí's maturity, in the Casa Batlló for instance, or even the Casa Milà.

But we are getting ahead of the story. The first building boom in Barcelona produced a great deal more than its stock exchange and the Saló de Cent. In terms of industrial fourteenth-century architecture, the greatest surviving example in the world stands just back from the Barcelona waterfront: the Drassanes or shipyards, a masterpiece of civil engineering built by the architect Arnau Ferre and finished in 1378, during the reign of Peter the Ceremonious—a set of long parallel bays made of brick, their tiled roofs carried on great diaphragm arches. In its plain and imposing spaces, the biggest vessels in the Mediterranean were built, right up to the end of the seventeenth century. A facsimile of one such vessel, the *Capitana,* or flagship, in which Don Juan of Austria led the Christians to victory over the Turks at Lepanto in 1571, occupies a whole bay: a sleek baroque war machine encrusted with gilt and red lacquer, 195 feet long, driven by fifty-eight oars each as thick as a telegraph pole and worked by nearly six hundred chained slaves. A mile away, in one of the chapels of the Cathedral, stands the justly celebrated "Christ of Lepanto," a wooden sculpture carved from an elm trunk, twisted in *contrapposto* in the form of an *s:* a miracle, the story goes, because the Redeemer saw a cannonball heading straight at him from a Turkish bow chaser and, with divinely quick reflexes, twisted out of its way.

Then the reign of Peter the Ceremonious produced some remarkable structures which, though they weren't religious, had a very strong ceremonial presence in the life of the city. Notably the huge banqueting hall, which sometimes served as a parliament in the 1370s, known as the Saló del Tinell. North of the Pyrenees, English and French Gothic architects focused on emphasizing the height of their structures, supporting the walls with flying buttresses. In Catalunya the opposite occurs. The wall remains earthbound, defined by mass. Or there is no wall—as in the Saló del Tinell, a tunnel which retains a ghost memory of the Pyrenean cave. The basic form of a medieval Catalan church is one big nave, no aisles, and a polygonal apse at one end with a choir at the other. Single-nave churches of this kind can be very wide indeed. One Catalan architectural historian pointed out that when a Catalan entered a long, narrow French cathedral nave he felt it lacked coziness, which medieval Catalans felt they had a right to expect from the *casa pairal de déu,* God's family house, where they gathered at the altar like brothers, sisters, and cousins at the llar de foc, the capacious and inviting fireplace—the cave, again.

Stone is not difficult to build high, because it is so strong in compression. But building wide introduces bending stresses, and these entail tension. And stone is weak in tension. Because we live in an age of steel and reinforced concrete, we take very wide spans for granted. In the fourteenth century, however, wide spans in stone were a marvel, and the Catalan architects were unsurpassed in their construction.

The widest vaulted nave in Europe (seventy-eight feet, only five feet narrower than the colossal barrel vault of St. Peter's in Rome) is that of the fourteenth-century Catedral de Girona in Catalunya.

Wide Gothic has its own external grandeur and interior drama, as the fourteenth-century Santa Maria del Pi (begun in 1322) abundantly shows. Its facade is almost bare of ornament, and even when its twelve niches were filled with sculptures (of which they were stripped long ago during some iconoclastic fit) it must have looked aggressively plain: a sheet of stone stretched between two engaged octagonal towers. Inside, the severity persists. The Pi's single nave confronts you all at once. Below the disk of the rose window, a choir is supported on a shallow stone arch that spans the whole width of the church. It is almost flat, for the fourteenth-century Catalan masons could build shallow arches that seem to defy the laws of bending stress. Today no modern architect would attempt such forms in stone without steel reinforcement.

Though undeniably grand, the Cathedral of Barcelona (not to be confused with Gaudí's incomplete Sagrada Família, which is not a cathedral but an "expiatory temple") is a gloomy building: heavy, cluttered, blackened. Its foundations go back to a Christian shrine of the fourth century A.D., built on what must have been part of the original Roman forum. Its most recent part is the one visitors see first: the facade, commissioned by a banking and railroad baron in the nineteenth century and designed by the local architect Josep Oriol I Mestres—its flamboyant design being based on drawings made four hundred years earlier by a French architect in Rouen. This design, though handsome, is clearly out of kilter with the much severer, tougher Gothic of the rest of the building and of the Old City in general.

For most people, I suspect, the most enjoyable part of the Cathedral is its cloister—a delicious Gothic oasis, its paths paved with the largely effaced tomb slabs of medieval worthies (including a court jester), with tall green palms, pools, cresses, and mosses everywhere on the fountains, and honking regiments of white geese. Whatever reason these birds have for being there—were their very distant ancestors installed as a replay of the sacred geese of the Roman capitol, since their territory is a transplanted colonial forum?—is lost in the mists of time.

Beyond much argument, the most beautiful Gothic church in Barcelona—or in Spain, some would insist—is Santa Maria del Mar. Certainly it is the one I always visit and consult first when I want to feel completely back in Barcelona. It stands at the bottom of the Ribera quarter, where the city meets the sea, and is essentially dedicated to the strong, traditionally thriving relation between Barcelona and its working citizens. That is why, without sentimentality, one loves it so: There is little trace of the aristocratic grandeur, the slightly condescending too-muchness, of "nobler" Spanish churches.

Ritual use of this site goes back a long way. The original church or shrine, of which no visible trace survives, may have been Barcelona's first episcopal seat at the time of Constantine, in the fourth century. Its construction began only a little later than the Pi's, in 1329, and took slightly more than half a century to complete.

Its first cult was dedicated to Santa Eulàlia, patroness of Barcelona, but when her relics were moved to the Cathedral a new and much bigger church began to rise on the site of the old, dedicated to Christ's mother in her role as patroness of mariners—Holy Mary of the Sea. That is why an ancient model of a deep-bellied *nef* or working caravel stands on its altar.

By now the Ribera quarter around the shrine was getting prosperous and its streets were named for specific guilds—Carrer del Argenteria (silversmithing), Carrer dels Sombrerers (hatmakers), and so on. Being on the sea's edge, the church was associated with haulers, porters, and the *bastaixos,* as longshoremen were called. All made heavy cash contributions to its building. On the main altar of Santa Maria del Mar are two squat stone relief carvings of stevedores carrying their loads. Not for nothing has Santa Maria always been viewed as a place made by workers for workers. According to the chronicles, most of the able-bodied male population of the Ribera gave it their labor and time for more than fifty years. Of its four great Gothic vaults, the last was closed in November 1383.

Massive, square, forthright, heavy, this is not lacy Gothic. Its imagery of shelter recalls, in equal measure, the caves of the Pyrenees and the fortress-churches of Cistercian Catalunya. But there is no more solemn architectural space in Spain. Granted, the interior of Santa Maria del Mar was considerably improved by the anticlericals and anarchists who, during the civil war, made a huge mound inside the nave of pews, wooden sculpture, and confessionals, even the incongruous baroque high altar, and set fire to it. The conflagration lasted eleven days, turned the church into a white-hot kiln, but, amazingly, failed to bring down its structure. Only the bones remain, but those bones are so beautiful that one cannot regret the loss of the ornament.

The plan of Santa Maria is basilican, a central nave with two flanking aisles that swing around behind the high altar to form a semicircular apse. Chapels are set between the counterfort stub walls that oppose the outward thrust of the roof. The nave columns, which rise to only a little more than half the nave's height, are plain octagons in section. From their thin capitals, hardly more than gilded rings, spring the ribs of the roof. These ribs are the plainest of stone pipes, and their linear definition against the surfaces of wall and vault is intensely moving in its purity and strictness. This spareness is emphasized by spacing, for the columns of Santa Maria del Mar are farther apart than those of any other Gothic church in Europe—about forty-three feet.

When I was a little Catholic boy I used to resent being forced to traipse to Mass on Sundays, because the Church of St. Mary Magdalen in Rose Bay, Sydney, like everything in it, was so boring and ugly with its atmosphere of sterile plaster-cast purity. To this day there is a certain shade of blue whose mincing pallidness I cannot endure; it is the color given to the Virgin's robe by the firm of Antonio Pellegrini & Fratelli, ecclesiastical decorators of Sydney. But I could (well, maybe) imagine remaining a good little Catholic if the church had been more like Santa Maria del Mar. Perhaps there should have been some anarchists around to burn the pious rubbish, although the sight of the column of smoke pouring upward into the Australian blue would have been too much for the bankers and brewers who had been to early Mass and were now immersed in their drives and chip shots on the nearby course of Royal Sydney Golf Club.

TWO

AFTER ITS BRILLIANT ACHIEVEMENTS IN THE FOURTEENTH century, could Barcelona sustain such cultural momentum? Alas, no, and the reasons were several. No city, however energetic, can be expected to keep up such a level for long. Fine buildings continued to be erected in Barcelona: the fifteenth- and sixteenth-century parts of the Palau de la Generalitat, the building on Plaça Sant Jaume that houses the government of the state of Catalunya, are among those which testify to that. There are also the beautiful *palaus* (palaces) and town houses of Carrer Montcada, a strikingly well-preserved street that goes from the corner of Santa Maria del Mar, across the

Carrer Princesa to the tiny Plaça Marcus, where the diminutive twelfth-century Capilla (Chapel) de Marcus still stands—the point from which, in the Middle Ages, most travelers heading north to France began their journey.

It is rarely possible to say where a very old town street began its existence, but Carrer Montcada is an exception: It was created from scratch in 1148, as a planned whole, by the last man to rule over Barcelona as a count-king before Catalunya's fusion with Aragon, Ramón Berenguer.

The buildings that defined Carrer Montcada in the twelfth century are all gone now, replaced, in the fifteenth to sixteenth centuries or later, by the palaces of the very rich, whose frowning street walls (no setbacks here for pedestrians) and squinting windows seem as unwelcoming, if not actually hostile, to the passerby as the clan *palazzi* on the narrow streets of Florence.

The typical palau was built between party walls and around an inner court, with storage and workrooms on the ground floor and a vaulted staircase, often richly decorated, leading to the living space and ceremonial rooms above. Having been recycled into museums and art galleries, most of them are now open to the public. The Palau Dalmases (No. 20, now the Omnium Cultural) has some fifteenth-century vaulting, but the main feature of its courtyard is the staircase, with finely carved seventeenth-century columns and a balustrade whose sharply inclined panels bear baroque allegories of Catalan sea trade and naval victory carved in marble in shallow relief. Neptune, with his attendant nymphs and sea horses, goes charging through the white stone foam—but uphill, following the pitch of the staircase at thirty degrees or so.

The Casa Cervelló-Giudice (No. 25, now the Galerie Maeght) was built by Catalans and purchased in the eighteenth century by a foreign trading family from Genoa. It has the best external courtyard staircase of all, its vaults carried on fifteenth-century stone columns so exaggeratedly slender that the slightest movement in the subsoil would have brought them down; on first sight you would think they were cast iron, not limestone.

There is not much baroque building in Barcelona, because the city's cultural history ran so opposite to that of Madrid; years of prosperity in one were almost always a time of recession in the other, what with ever increasing competition from Castile, overseas pressure, costly civil wars and reckless policies of urban expansion that Barcelona's own capital base could not sustain. The period of the sixteenth to mid-nineteenth century enclosed, for Castile, its so-called golden century, its *siglo d'oro.* Not in Catalunya, where the same period was known as the *Decadencia,* in which little worthy of pride or remark happened in the arts of painting, poetry, music, or architecture, and the power of the city itself contracted even as Madrid's was bursting out into worldwide hegemony. There was no Catalan Velázquez and, even though he recuperated in Barcelona for a time and praised its life and customs extravagantly, no Catalan Cervantes either. In Castile, baroque and realism are almost all; in Catalunya they are nearly nothing. Barcelona is very short, for instance, of fine neoclassic buildings from the eighteenth and early nineteenth centuries. One good group stands on the seafront, the Porxos d'en Xifré, or Mr. Xifré's porches—Xifré, having become rich on the colonial transatlantic trade in slaves and coffee, wished like many other indianos to leave a mark on his home city. (It seems fitting that his name, in Catalan, meant "number.") It contains a well-known restaurant, the Seven Doors, solid and reliable if not the best in Barcelona, which performs for the city some of the functions of La Coupole in Paris or Balthazar in New York—the production of copious amounts of good vernacular food for a large clientele both of locals and of tourists. It is a trustworthy place and worth visiting, even if you may no longer feel any special desire to sit at the table where, a brass plaque still informs the visitor, Ernest Hemingway once ate.

Why this should be considered a gastronomic recommendation, the Lord only knows.

The Ramblas holds two neoclassic palaces, the only other ones of interest in Barcelona. One (Ramblas, No. 99) is the Palau de la Virreina, and the other Palau Moja (Ramblas, No. 118). The Virreina is a pile of epic and bulbous proportions, built by the extremely corrupt captain-general of Chile, Manuel d'Amat i de Junyent, who in 1761 had received from his king the juiciest of all colonial plums, the viceroyalty of Peru, whose chief perk was unsupervised control of the richest silver deposit in the known world, the fabled mines of Potosí, an invitation to plunder that no red-blooded, sticky-fingered Catalan could possibly refuse.

It would be cruel and unusual punishment to subject the reader to an account of the various civil wars and disturbances that weakened Catalunya on the way to and during the siglo d'oro, but they should at least be indicated.

By 1462 there had begun a confused melee between the monarchy and the ruling class which ruptured most of the long-standing contracts between the throne, the Generalitat, and Barcelona's city government. This resulted in 1479 in the emergence of Ferdinand II (the Catholic) as ruler of Catalunya. Ferdinand then married the future Isabel I of Castile; who, on ascending the Castilian throne, wrote an end to the long independence of Catalunya that had begun, six hundred years before, with Wilfred the Hairy.

Then came the Reapers' War (1640-1652), a drawn-out and slow-moving bloodbath started by peasant laborers in revolt against Habsburg rule.

Most catastrophic of all was the entry of Catalunya into the War of the Spanish Succession against the Bourbons, whom it could not defeat. This war started in 1701 and by the summer of 1714 all of Catalunya had been taken, except for Barcelona itself, which fought on alone, deserted by its allies.

The city had only about ten thousand soldiers, a force soon whittled down by gunfire, famine, and disease. Their resistance was anguished and stubborn, but it could not last long. Barcelona surrendered to the Bourbon army, led by James Stuart, duke of Berwick, on September 11, 1714, a date which might well be remembered as ignominious (as 9/11 now is in the United States), but which for some perverse reason is still celebrated as the national day of Catalunya.

The legend of eighteenth-century Bourbon tyranny still lives on, but its life is merely vestigial. True, there were vengeful Castilians who would have liked to see Barcelona razed and its citizens punished with the utmost severity short of death. But Felipe was not an exceptionally vengeful man, and once Berwick's men had hanged some resisters and demolished some buildings to make their point, the Catalans settled down quite comfortably to do business with their conquerors, and prospered from it.

The worst thing the Bourbons did to Barcelona was to flatten hundreds of its buildings, mostly houses and shops, and erect a series of walls across these cleared sites, to turn it into an enormous fort: the Ciutadella, or Citadel. As a result, the military installations of the city covered almost as much land as its civilian and commercial buildings; it was given new and vastly stronger walls, which left it no room to grow. Since living space in *barris* like the Ribera was already tight and a breeding ground for pestilence and misery, this was bitterly resented by the citizens. Barcelona's great priest-poet, Jacint Verdaguer, looked back on these humiliations from a much later time in the 1880s:

> *The happiest quarter of Barcelona is erased*
> *like a number drawn in the sand, on the beach.*
> *When, like water drained away, no trace remains*
> *of these stones, the bones of the beloved city,*
> *they build a fortress,*
> *the ill-fated and hateful Citadel,*

born in Barcelona like erysipelas
in the middle of a lovely face.

The smashing down of the Ribera quarter, symbol of
the tough spirit of the Barcelona workingman, settled
deep into popular memory. Its scars humiliated every
Barcelonan, and the Bourbon muralles, the new walls
that clamped the monstrous outgrowth of the Citadel to
the offended body of the city, were loathed as much as
the Citadel itself. Probably not until the Berlin Wall
would any imposed structure be so hated by those who
lived in its shadow. The walls freighted every planning
decision, every opinion, with extra meaning. Were you
for democracy or the military? Catalan independence or
Madrid centrality? Church or State? Your view of the
muralles would tell. They were an absolutely clear symbol of where "progressive" ideas of social administration
might be pointing. All "progressives" and Catalanists,
though the two were not necessarily the same, agreed on
that point. Before the city could return to its true self,
before it could reforge its identity, it had to get rid of
the muralles. An easy thing to say, but difficult to do.

Yet it was done—eventually, and with immense
effort. In the meantime, however, more misfortunes
awaited Barcelona. The summer of 1835 brought a
blaze of violent anticlericalism to Barcelona's always

unstable working class, fanned by liberal extremists in reaction against the absolute monarchists and the Carlists. Ferdinand VII, the ultrareactionary Bourbon monarch, had died in 1833. Late in his life he had compared himself to the cork in a bottle of beer: Once it was pulled, he said, the liquid would foam out everywhere. So it proved to do. The next in line for the throne had been his daughter, the future Isabel II. The idea of being ruled by this child queen through a regent horrified many Spanish conservatives, including the late Fernando's brother, Carlos María Isidro de Borbon, another extreme reactionary. His supporters, calling themselves the Carlists, wanted him for their king and refused to contemplate, let alone accept, a female heir to the throne. The result was a bloody, on-again-off-again battle between the Carlists on one hand and liberals and constitutionalists on the other. Barcelona's citizen militia stood behind the liberals. The Church, with equal fervor, supported the Carlists. This converted Barcelona into a tinderbox and in 1835 there was an orgy of anticlerical violence and arson which became known as the Cremada dels Convents, the Burning of the Convents.

Supposedly, and indeed quite possibly, it began with the hysteria of the crowd at a bullfight in Barcelona, enraged by the poor quality of the corrida. But it rapidly engulfed the city, gutting scores of church buildings—among them, medieval masterpieces such as the thirteenth- to fourteenth-century church and convent of the Carme, which ranked with Santa Maria del Mar in architectural importance. The rage of workers found a second target in big business. On August 6, demonstrating against the mechanization of craft work, a crowd of the unemployed burned down the new Bonaplata works, Spain's first steam factory and the pride of Catalan industry.

Then, after the fires, came the Mendizábal Laws. Juan Álvarez (1790-1853), a radical liberal who from 1835 was Isabel II's minister of finance, saw as his chief duty the task of opening the Spanish economy and getting investment moving again. He, therefore, took what was probably the most daring step in the entire history of the real estate business, in Spain or anywhere else.

The biggest landlord in Barcelona (or in the rest of Spain) was the Church, and Mendizábal confiscated its properties, forcing them to be sold at auction. Thus four-fifths of the Church lands inside the walls of Barcelona were snapped up by eager secular clients. This saved the city from the moribund hand of the Church—a traumatic excision, but an essential one.

It still amazes me how much of nineteenth-century Barcelona, and how many of my favorite places within the Barri Gòtic, were built on sites cleared under the

Mendizábal Laws. Francesc Daniel Molina's great residential square, the Plaça Reial just off the Ramblas, is one. Everyone has at least one sad song of a lost real estate opportunity. Mine, which I feel like morosely humming whenever I stop in one of the bars of Plaça Reial for a cold beer on a hot day, or (even more sharply) when I go to visit my architect friends Beth Galí and Oriol Bohigas in their apartment above, is the lodgings in Plaça Reial that I never had the sense to secure.

Back in the 1970s this beautiful complex—planned like one of the residential squares of Paris, and in this respect almost unique among the places of Barcelona— was sadly rundown, the haunt of junkies and bedraggled whores, its tall shutters hanging awry, its stucco cracked, its lofty fourteen-foot apartment ceilings in miserable condition. You could have bought one of those ruinous palaces for next to nothing. Others did. I did not. Regret and sadness, especially since the fabric of the square, with its fountains and early Gaudí cast-iron streetlamps (cast iron being the bronze of nineteenth-century Barcelona), was so elegantly restored by Federico Correa a few years later.

Another spot nearby, more precious to me even than Plaça Reial, is the Mercat de Sant Antoni, the Market of St. Anthony, just off the other side of the Ramblas but a little uptown, the official name, which of course no one ever uses for that stupendous civic institution which everyone calls the Boqueria.

It is the hub and heart of both Barcelona's gastronomy and its everyday eating. Its site was originally occupied by the sixteenth-century convent of Sant Josep and the fourteenth-century one of Santa Maria. Hang me for a gluttonous atheist if you will, but compared to the increase of human happiness afforded by this great market, the loss of a couple of convents is nothing.

The Boqueria stands at the edge of the Ramblas, which makes it easy for buyers to reach from the Old City but difficult for vendors, who with their carts and donkey loads of goods had to negotiate the crowded and constricted maze of the Raval.

For any serious lover of food—which most Catalans aggressively are—there is no other place in the world quite like the Boqueria, that vast covered space crammed with stalls that display just about everything short of human flesh that could conceivably be eaten, from skinned rabbits (their moist eyes still peering reproachfully at the hardhearted shopper) to soft brown hills of newly shot but unplucked partridges, neatly tied fagots of fat white Girona asparagus, frozen packages of fiendishly expensive but irresistible *angullas* or baby eels. One stall sells twenty kinds of olives and ten of capers, another a dozen kinds of *jamón*

Serrano, the cured mountain ham whose quality ranges all the way upstairs from good-ordinary to the exquisite, almost buttery *pata negra,* and *jabugo*. The central ring of the Boqueria is given over to fresh fish and shellfish in a thousand guises; a dozen stalls compete for the attention of those who want baccala or salt cod, that staple of Catalan cuisine; there are more kinds of sausage, fresh and cured, than there are poets in New Jersey, and their rich, fatty, smoky flavors induce deeper reveries. And this does not begin to enumerate the vegetables and fruit, all new, fresh, and at the top of their season. One would cross an ocean for the *habitas* or baby fava beans, and another for those small crisp infantas of the lettuce kingdom, the tightly clenched heads of the *cogollons de Tudela* which, cut in half lengthways, anointed with olive oil and topped with an *x* of not-too-salty anchovy fillets, make the best salad in the world. And then the cheeses. And the yogurts. And the herbs and, in season, the stupendous arrays of fresh mushrooms. And the Catalan badinage of the white-coated women behind the counters, the red-knuckled fishwives brandishing their enormous, glittering, crescent-shape choppers, which look medieval but, honed to a razor edge, are capable of dazzlingly precise feats of dissection. (Yours for about twenty-five dollars at one of the kitchenware shops along the edge of the Boqueria, though sneaking such a formidable weapon past the antiterrorist guards at the airport is your problem, too.) If there were a grocery, butcher, and fishmonger attached to the Garden of Eden, in which one could sample what terrestrial food tasted like before the fall of man, it would be something like the Boqueria. *"Non si pasce in cibo mortale / Chi si pasce in cibo celeste,"* sings Mozart's Commendatore, rather snottily, to Don Giovanni; but personally, if I could get it at the Boqueria, I would be more than happy to keep nourishing myself on mortal food and let the holy manna go rot. Since Les Halles so tragically decamped from the center of Paris, there has been no publicly accessible food market in the world with quite the same character, variety, and beauty of produce as the Boqueria.

All this is perhaps hard on the gastronomically inclined traveler, who may not cook in his or her hotel room. My own solution, a victimless crime in which I have not yet been detected, is always to take *something* back to New York; a *fuet*, say, or whip, one of those oxtail-thin sausages; a good lump of fresh Manchego cheese, or a kilo of jamón Serrano on the bone. And the person behind the counter in the Boqueria will always vacuum-wrap it for you in stout plastic, so that the airport dogs at Kennedy can't get a scent.

But I digress. Or do I? To me, food seems so entirely central to any experience of Barcelona that I cannot think of the city without it. Catalan food has a directness, an unfussed and fundamental virtue, that is hard to find elsewhere, except in Italy and certain parts of France. It is one of the world's great cuisines, and although some recent celebrity chefs like Ferran Adria have volatilized it into the sort of nouvelle performance excess that food editors dote on, it is on the whole free from the kind of over-elaboration that makes cooking feel artsy and decadent. It has never forgotten its peasant and artisanal roots. A too "refined" paella, for instance, one without the *cremada* or burned undercrust where the rice met the iron, would be no paella at all. You know, when gazing fork in hand upon a *butifarra*—the fresh pork sausage of Catalunya—with its attendant white beans, that you are looking at the Truth and, better yet, on the point of cutting into its blistered and slightly blackened skin, that you are about to taste the Truth of sausagehood, too.

An institution of a very different and somewhat less democratic kind also rose on the Ramblas in 1847, not far from the Boqueria, dedicated to the ears rather than the stomach. This was the Gran Teatre del Liceu, Barcelona's opera house, the classical counterpart and predecessor to the Palau de la Música Catalana. It stands where a convent of Trinitarian friars had once been. And so one might continue. All in all, one may fairly say that Mendizábal saved the economic life, and to no small extent the cultural life, too, of the city. So is there a plaza named after him? A wide and noble street? Not so much as an alley, alas. For this we must thank the malignant influence of a vengeful Church. The ultra-conservative clergy of nineteenth-century Barcelona would no more have consented to naming anything after the liberal confiscator of their property than the rab-binate of Jerusalem would have permitted a Goebbels Street. But there is a solitary little Bar Mendizábal in the Carrer del Junta del Comerç, right behind the Boqueria. Its fiercely socialist owner would not for a moment consider changing its name.

The Bourbons's great gift to Barcelona was the Ramblas, that sublime and raffish avenue whose name means, in the original Arabic, "riverbeds." Its first form appears in a city map published in 1740—a wide, uneven, and slightly bent street running north-northeast from a point near the harborside Drassanes to a gate in the northern ramparts of the new muralles. It was merely the fossil, the filled-in bed, of Barcelona's western stream, the Cagallel, which served both as moat and as sewer. By the eighteenth century this foul trickle was so clogged with rubbish and ordure that it was filled and driven underground, a burial it long continued to resist. But it emerged as a more or less straight avenue, very different in form to the intestinal windings of the Old City. This straightness was imposed by authority, which wanted a clear line of fire for its grapeshot in the event of riots and disturbances. It became the first true modern avenue in Catalunya, and very beautiful it is, with its double line of mottled, cream-trunked plane trees. Today, for most people, the Ramblas *is* Barcelona. Here are the flower stalls, bursting with gaudy color. (Catalans are not known for the subtlety of their flower arrangements.) Here are the *tiendas* selling birds, from finches and squeaking budgerigars to lugubrious-looking, slightly moth-eaten toucans with their enormous, saberlike bills. (Every so often one of the green Amazonian parrots, or more rarely one of the *aras* or red macaws, escapes from its cage and flies off across the city like a brightly plumed comet, to join the refugee colonies of other parrots whose ancestors likewise escaped from the Ramblas and now lurk, screeching and flapping, in the trees of the Parc de la Ciutadella.) Here are the "human statues" poised immobile on their crates, bizarre and infrangibly silent. Here, above all, are the crowds: workers, shoppers, gawking tourists, *flaneurs,* whores, and thieves, the rich and the wretched of the Earth, moving in unending streams and eddies up and down the sloping pavement of the Ramblas, across the huge mosaic decorations laid into the footpath by the assistants of Joan Miró decades ago, engaged in the ever serious process of manifesting themselves as Barcelonans, real or temporary. The Ramblas is and always will be one of the great, seedy, absorbing theaters of Spain, or for that matter of Europe.

GIVEN BARCELONA'S PROPENSITY FOR COMMITTING ITSELF to the flames and then rising from them like some clumsily singed phoenix, it's hardly surprising that ideological violence in one form or another has marked the city so deeply. It was a place where socialist theory and fantasy bit early and would always stay close to the surface, well into the twentieth century—as the civil war would show.

One of the exemplary figures in the modernization of Barcelona—though hardly a typical one, being far too unusual and gifted a man to be called that—was an inventor named Narcis Monturiol. I had never heard of him, of course, before spending time in the city. He had not, in fact, changed the physical face of the city at all.

But one day in the mid-1970s, I was strolling along a narrow street full of antique shops in the Old City, when an oddity in a window stopped me. It was a model of a ship, but like no ship I had ever seen. It was about thirty inches long and made, precisely and with care, of brass and copper. Its general form was fishlike. Though it lacked fins it had a shallow cloven tail, which served both as rudder and propeller guard. It had no deck, but what looked like a primitive hemisphere of a conning tower surrounded by a railing. It had fish-eye portholes and a glass nose, and set into its hull was a quite large clock, about five inches in diameter. All this suggested that the curio had once been a model of a real craft of some kind, and that it had been well-enough known as an image to demand no special explanation.

It sat on a plinth, which bore a darkened brass plate. It read, in Spanish: ICTÍNEO, PRODUCT OF THE GENIUS OF NARCIS MONTURIOL.

This was worth a look.

With some difficulty—I had no more than a smidgen of spoken Catalan back then—the shop owner conveyed to me, politely but unambiguously, that he could scarcely believe that I, seemingly an educated man despite my linguistic deficiencies, had never so much as heard of the great Monturiol, inventor of the Catalan submarine and, as such, the father of all later submarines. He recommended a visit to Plaça de Catalunya, at the top of the Ramblas, where I could gaze on the monument to Monturiol by the contemporary sculptor Josep Subirachs, best known as the sculptor-in-chief to the Sagrada. And sure enough, the monument was there, a bigger cousin of the brass submarine clock in the window of the antique shop, clockless of course, and poised in the act of swimming through a formalized bronze grotto.

I thought of my ("my," already!) submarine clock, and was filled with cupidity. I am not a collector. But occasionally something strikes me with its curiosity, its sheer oddity. *I want, I want ...* and yet I didn't hightail it back to the store that afternoon. Something, I forget what, got in the way. Maybe I wasn't feeling aggressive enough to bargain, which all *forasters* (outsiders) should ruthlessly do. In any event, I didn't go back for two days, and when I did the velvet-covered table on which *Ictíneo* had reposed was empty except for a couple of porcelain shepherds. Apparently someone else in Barcelona lusted after a submarine clock. Could there be two such people in a city of less than three million? Apparently so. I had lost my chance.

Disconsolate, I decided to turn the knife in the self-inflicted wound by reading about Narcis Monturiol and the *Ictíneo*. It turned out to be a story of considerable

pathos which casts a light—oblique, yes, but bright—
on Barcelona itself. As an inventor, Narcis Monturiol i
Estarrol (1819-1885) was not a successful hero, like
Henry Ford or Thomas Edison. He was altogether interesting, though, as a *failed* hero: one of the potential gods
of early technology who didn't quite make it, despite a
certain indubitable genius.

Nineteenth-century Catalans took vast pride in
being first in any technology. And if not first in the
world, which they never were, or in Europe, which sel-
dom happened, then first in Spain—a lot less difficult,
since Spanish technology and practical science were so
far behind that of most other countries.

By the 1860s Barcelona was first among the industrialized cities of Spain, with twice the manufacturing
capacity as all the rest of the country put together.

This was due to textiles. Barcelona was fourth in the
world in the manufacture of cotton goods, after England,
France, and the United States. In Spain, the city had a
monopoly of machine spinning and weaving, and was
the Manchester of the south. This mechanization came
from what the Spanish called the *selfactina* or self-acting
machine loom, which came into use in Spain in 1832,
half a century after its invention in England. By 1861
Catalunya had 9,695 such looms, and their use fostered
Barcelona's second industry, mechanical engineering. By

the end of the 1840s the big cotton and silk companies of Barcelona included La Fabril Igualadina (1847), La Espana Industrial (1847), Güell, Ramis i Cia (1848), and the Batlló Brothers (1849). By 1862, the engines of the Catalan textile industry accounted for more than a third of Spain's steam power; raw cotton was Catalunya's biggest import; and the industrial barons, especially the Güells and Batllós, would be the emergent patrons of a new architectural style.

The first daily newspaper to be printed in Spain (and the second in Europe after the *Times*) was *El Brusi,* the old *Diario de Barcelona.* The train from Barcelona to Sarrià, opened in 1863, was the second metropolitan railroad (after London's) in the world. The first city-to-city train in Spain connected Barcelona to Mataró in 1848. Barcelona had the country's first cinema and its first public phone, and ran its first airline (to Majorca).

And being the industrial leader of Spain, it was also the chief incubator of labor unrest in southern Europe.

Its politics were riven by anarchism and terrorism. Given the enormous power of the Catholic Church and its embrace of the most right-wing elements in Spanish capitalism, leftist ideology—particularly anarchism, which appealed to disillusioned young Catholics because of its promise of irrational, "pie in the sky" justice—had the ground prepared for it: The last years of the nineteenth century in Barcelona unrolled to the sound of terrorist bomb explosions, and the Setmana Tragica or Tragic Week of 1909 in which, once again, the city was burned by its citizens, made Barcelona the world capital of politically inspired violence. It also hosted Europe's first Workers' Congress, staged the first general strike south of the Pyrenees, and so on.

One strand in the Catalan left, however, was inherently peaceful and wished only to secede from capitalism and form its own ideal society, inside Spain if possible, outside if necessary. Its spiritual godfather was a Frenchman, Étienne Cabet (1785-1856). Prosecuted for publishing a socialist sheet, he fled to England in 1834, and there came in contact with the benignly utopian manufacturer and social theorist Robert Owen. He labored in that hatchery of a million schemes, the British Museum Reading Room, devouring texts on republican brotherhood: François-Emile Babeuf, Charles Fourier, Owen himself. Cabet was not a mad visionary like Fourier. His eccentricity took the mild form of seeing Christ's Sermon on the Mount for what it clearly was: an early socialist tract. It was based on "gentleness and charity." "We find in it the source of all the modern systems that now shake the world ... there is no gulf between the social teachings of the Gospels and those of socialism."

The result of this belief was Cabet's text *A Voyage to Icaria,* 1839, in which he laid out a plan for an ideal society (Icaria) in the form of imagined dialogues between an English aristocrat (based on Owen) and a young, exiled artist (Cabet). To most people today, Cabet's Icaria would be a hellish place, a dystopia without free will, where everything from diet to publishing is controlled by the state, and no irritants, especially no byproducts of the competitive instinct, are allowed. Cabet's vision of intellectual life in Icaria is like an even more sinister version of the toxic vogue for political correctness on American campuses, or the witless loathing of elitism in Australian journalism in the late twentieth century.

Cabet's ideas were ignored in France. But a small number of Catalan intellectuals were excited by them, and his chief disciple among these Catalans in the late 1840s and '50s was an attractive figure—Narcis Monturiol, socialist, editor, mechanical inventor, and pioneer of the submarine, who hailed from the fishing port of Figueres and is still regarded there as its favorite son.

In 1847 he and a few other earnest progressives formed an Icarian group in Barcelona. Its anthem ran:

> *Desde hoy todos los hombres son hermanos*
> *ni siervo se conoce, ni seño.*

Marchemos, O marchemos Icarianos,
tendiendo el estandarte del Amor!

From today, all men are brothers,
there will be no slave or master
Let us march, O march onward, Icarians,
holding up the banner of Love!

"The Universal Era," declared the group's news sheet, "begins with the foundation of Icaria. January 20, 1848, is the moment fixed for the regeneration of the World."

This was the date on which Étienne Cabet sailed for America to found an Icarian community on land purchased sight unseen from a real estate shark, northwest of New Orleans, near Shreveport, Louisiana. It was sand and swamp, and only mosquitoes and venomous snakes flourished there. Monturiol did not go with the first group, believing that twenty thousand people would join it. Only sixty-nine did. Some, guessing what lay before them, committed suicide. The remainder trekked north to Nauvoo, Illinois, and founded a new settlement there, which lasted a few more years. Monturiol never got to join them. Harried by his resentful disciples, Cabet died of heartbreak in Nauvoo in 1856.

That was the end of Icaria, which survived only as the name given to an industrial slum in Barcelona. Around 1900 the city fathers renamed it Poblenou ("New Town"). One broad street, which not inappropriately stops dead at the gates of the Old Cemetery, retained the name of Avinguda d'Icaria. Then in 1992 the Olympic Village, built for the games in Barcelona, was named Nova Icaria—an extraordinarily silly notion, since Olympic contests are about nothing *but* competition, which the original Icarians had sworn to eliminate from their future world.

So the image of invention and industrial newness floated over Catalunya like a liberating angel. Inventing the submarine belonged to such an order of things, whether the submarine really worked or not. Monturiol was not a bit discouraged by the evaporation of Icaria. It just put the emphasis back where his talents required it to be: in exploration through technology. "The poles of the Earth," he declared, "the depths of the oceans, the upper regions of the air: these three conquests are undoubtedly reserved for the near future ... such is the task I have taken on."

Europeans had dreamed of probing the depths of the sea in controlled underwater voyages since antiquity. Early on, experiments bore some fruit: In 1801, for instance, the American inventor Robert Fulton made a five-hour descent to 160 feet off Brest in France, in a craft named the *Nautilus* (whose name Jules Verne appropriated), driven by a hand-cranked propeller.

But subs with engines for underwater running did not exist until Monturiol produced the second model of his *Ictíneo,* a name made up of the Greek words for "fish" and "ship." The first version was only twenty-three feet long and displaced eight tonnes. She was driven by four crank-turning aquanauts, and one of Monturiol's colleagues, perhaps his devoted wife who had been his constant companion in triumph and ill luck, made a flag: a gold star shedding light on a branch of red coral, with the Latin motto *"Plus intra, plus extra,"* meaning (roughly) "Far down! Far out!" *Ictíneo I* cost 100,000 pesetas, burdening Monturiol with a debt from which he never escaped.

It did not deter him. The trials of *Ictíneo I* in Barcelona harbor had been watched by many enthusiastic Catalans. Her dives were short, because she could only carry the air that was in her small hull at normal pressure. But the spectacle was enough to make her inventor a local celebrity, a Catalan Leonardo. Officials promised to bring the sovereign, Isabel II, to watch and witness. Discouraged by the pooh-bahs of her own Admiralty, she never came, but over the next few years Monturiol took his ship down again some fifty times. Meanwhile he was busy planning and building *Ictíneo II,* at fifty-six feet more than twice as long as the first model, and powered for undersea running by an ingenious chemical-reaction engine that did not require air to raise steam and actually created free, breathable oxygen. She was designed to dive to a hundred feet and stay down for seven and a half hours. Her design was brilliantly innovative but the research cost Monturiol and his socialist comrades a fortune—and, by their standards, not a small one.

They made more than a dozen demonstration dives in *Ictíneo II* over the next few years. She worked perfectly, the most advanced undersea craft ever devised. Further developed, she would have been a huge strategic gift to the Spanish navy. (What could a small fleet of *Ictíneos,* suitably armed, have done to Admiral Dewey's battle squadron at that fateful engagement off Manila, which sealed the doom of the Spanish Empire?) As it was, all she got was a lot of press, with illustrations of *Ictíneo* hunting for precious red coral and engaging in combat with other subs. The torpid naval ministry in Madrid merely sent its compliments, not contracts or money. The mill owners and iron magnates of Barcelona only eyed the big fish with curiosity. In 1868 Monturiol's creditors foreclosed on him and seized *Ictíneo II.* Having no commercial value as a ship, she was broken up and sold as scrap.

The failure of his dream broke Monturiol's heart. Bankrupt and depressed, he eventually died in 1885, in his son-in-law's house at Sant Martí de Provençals.

By then he was a forgotten man in Catalunya, but it may be that his old fame had spread to France. In the 1860s Jules Verne was plowing through his research for *Twenty Thousand Leagues Under the Sea.* Was Captain Nemo, commander of the supersub *Nautilus,* inspired by Narcis Monturiol? It seems unlikely that Verne would *not* have heard of Monturiol, or admired the man's noble single-mindedness in adversity. Granted, Captain Nemo (whose name is the same in Latin as Ulysses' chosen Greek name of *Outis,* "no one") is unlike the mild Catalan. He is hugely rich, Monturiol desperately poor; Monturiol bent on brotherhood, Nemo on cosmic vengeance.

And yet there are similarities, too. Both men are utopians. When the narrator suggests that Nemo might be too rich to transcend his own capitalist interests, the captain fiercely turns on him: "Who told you that I do not make good use of it? Do you think I do not know that there are suffering races and oppressed beings on this earth...? Do you not *understand?*" From which Professor Aronnax concludes that "whatever the motive that had forced him to seek independence under the sea ... his heart still beat for the sufferings of humanity." The

Nautilus, ranging free beyond the reach of land governments, is of course a country in itself and may be seen as a parallel to self-sustaining utopian states like Icaria.

The second main phase of Barcelona's self-creation, after the Old City had filled up, was the Eixample, which in Catalan means "enlargement"—the Cerdà plan, as it was called after its designer, a Catalan planner named Ildefons Cerdà i Sunyer (1815-1876). It was one thing to demolish the muralles, those much hated emblems of Bourbon power over Barcelona. Getting rid of them was, as one observer noted, "the most ardent desire of every Barcelonan, the most popular and discussed idea in the country." It was certainly not the sole property of the Left and its civic ambitions. But when the city burst out of its stone corset, what would be its controlling form? That was the big question facing Cerdà and everyone else who thought about Barcelona.

The first step was to destroy the walls. It took time. Whole sections of the Roman walls of the Old City have survived to this day. So have parts of the medieval walls. But of the Bourbon muralles, absolutely nothing remains, and the hated Citadel was transformed into a park whose best known occupant, for the last two decades, was a much loved albino gorilla named Floquet de Neu, or Snowflake, that recently died. I never laid eyes on Snowflake. But Doris did, once.

Cerdà had studied civil engineering in Madrid. But his social convictions came out of his experience of working-class conditions in Barcelona: the overcrowding, the disease, the dreadful suffering. He was an indefatigable researcher, and his first book, *A Statistical Monograph on the Working Class of Barcelona in 1856* was the first systematic effort anyone had made to study the living and working space of the city. It was very detailed and deeply alarming. While the bards of the early Renaixenca were warbling nostalgically about the need to bring back the glories of the Catalan Middle Ages, it was clear that in terms of hygiene and social services the ordinary working folk of the city had never escaped them. The more abuses Cerdà found, the more indignantly radical he became. The future would be a race between the betterment of Barcelona's working and housing conditions, and the social implosion of the city. How to prevent the latter was the theme of Cerdà's next, and principal, book, *General Theory of Urbanization, and … the Reform and Expansion of Barcelona,* published (after many delays) in 1867. A new world was coming, Cerdà declared; "We lead a new life, functioning in a new way; old cities are no more than an obstacle."

The Eixample or New City would be the apotheosis of reason, the triumph of the grid, a perfect undifferentiated fabric. Cerdà would hardly have thought of planning something like the New City without the prototype of Baron Haussmann's restructuring of Paris before his eyes. But there was a huge difference. Haussmann had to destroy the old Paris, whereas Cerdà had to destroy nothing. He was going to enlarge Barcelona by laying a uniform grid on what was, except for a few villages (Sarrià, Gràcia, and others), a blank slate. Nothing stood in the way of the grid. Thus, a utopian designer's dream.

That was perfect for Cerdà, a utopian socialist, deeply affected by French ideas of ideal community. The lost egalitarian fantasies of Étienne Cabet, summed up in the ideal city of equal cells, imagined as Icaria, underwrite Cerdà's grid. Cerdà thought of each of these blocks as a social cross section; there would be no "good" and no "bad" end of town. He envisioned an absolutely regular grid covering a land surface of nearly nine square kilometers. Actually, it could be expanded forever. Each district of four hundred blocks (twenty by twenty) would have its own hospital, park, and so forth, and would be further divided into hundred-block units and then into barris of twenty-five blocks, each with its own schools and daycare centers. Only about a third of each block (five thousand square meters) would be built on;

the rest would be patio and green space, with at least a hundred trees.

But many such refinements went by the board, thanks to developers' greed and graft and laziness, particularly during the long Franco era. The Eixample today is far denser and higher, more chaotic in texture and generally more oppressive than Ildefons Cerdà could ever have imagined. Cerdà designed his standard block with 710,000 feet of built floor space and a maximum height of some fifty-seven feet, later increased to sixty-five. Over the next century developers managed to increase this fourfold, to three million square feet per block; an urbanistic disaster, a fraud on the public, and a travesty of Cerdà's plan.

Even so, the Eixample is one of the most interesting urban areas in Europe. It grew very slowly; not until the mid-1870s, when the Catalan economy entered the boom decade known as the *febre d'or* or gold fever, did the blocks begin in earnest to fill up. By 1872 there were about a thousand residential structures in the Eixample and some twenty thousand people were living in them. Its streets were mostly unpaved strips of dust. There was little storm-water drainage, so that after deluges the water collected in standing pools on its vacant lots, breeding swarms of *Anopheles* mosquitoes which presented Barcelona with epidemic malaria. In 1888 the report of a sanitary engineer named Pere Garcia Faria made it plain that the Eixample was, from the viewpoint of sanitation, just as bad as the Old City and possibly even worse. The ideal housing had failed through the greed of landlords, who had turned the houses into "veritable slums, in which the Barcelonan family is imprisoned." Health had caused the demolition of the muralles. But thirty years later, the Eixample was still swept by epidemics of cholera, TB, and typhoid, against which the authorities seemed powerless. And strangely enough—or perhaps not so strangely—the design of the Eixample found only limited favor with those who might have been Cerdà's backers, the next generation of modernist architects. Some of them, notably Josep Puig i Cadafalch, loathed the New City and made no secret of it, though its buildings are now considered by many to be among its jewels. Puig derided its "sacred monotony": "nothing equals it, except in the most vulgar cities of South America." There was much, much more. Everything that would in the future be said against the Eixample's heirs, from Le Corbusier's "radiant city" to Oscar Niemeyer's Brasília, was already said against their common ancestor the Eixample. All critics felt that leaving the planning of a city to Cerdà, a socialist, was a big mistake. And not all the criticisms of its monotony were without justice. What saves the Eixample are its star buildings, and the exhilarating processional quality of some of its streets, notably Passeig de Gràcia. But it is not really a place to walk in, as is the Old City: Its plan lacks the charm of surprise, of urban respiration through changes of angle and scale that the older and more organic cities of Europe provide.

The three decades after the Burning of the Convents in 1835 were difficult times for Barcelona. The sites of razed convents stayed empty, and there was rarely enough public money to build on spots confiscated by the Mendizábal Laws. The Old City was jammed. The New City was essentially unbuilt. Only the Ramblas had been developed in the previous half century, and this, not Passeig de Gràcia (which had not yet turned into the magnificent boulevard it is today), was Barcelona's social spine, with its plane trees, restaurants, and cafés. The most important new building on it, which opened with pomp around mid-century, was not far from Plaça Reial, the residential square just off the Ramblas where much of its clientele resided. This was the opera house, or Gran Teatre del Liceu.

It was a peculiarity of Catalan taste that the city had practically no time for anything but Italian opera. Symphonic works? Instrumental pieces? Forget it. *Bon gust* (proper taste) for most of the nineteenth century dictated that even Beethoven's *Fifth,* written in 1808 and still considered harsh and novel, was not performed in Barcelona until 1881. But opera, so long as it was Italian, was a different matter. Starting in the spring of 1847 with Verdi's *Giovanna D'Arco,* the new Liceu served up a solid diet of it for fourteen years, until the opera house burned to the ground (between performances) in 1861. This so mobilized public loyalty to the art that the Liceu opened a subscription fund and with incredible rapidity was open and playing again in only a year. The reconstruction by Josep Oriol i Mestres was if possible even more splendiferous than the original, featuring acres of yellow-and-white marble, gilt, stucco, and bronze, and a ceiling aswirl with painted cartouches.

Barcelona was not yet a huge city, and its life at the top, both social and philanthropic, was dominated by perhaps twenty clans, most of them owing their fortunes to nineteenth-century industries. The Güells were to these as the Rothschilds were to the financial baronies of France, though the Güells were not Jews. If you were rich you did not absolutely have to be an opera buff to win respect. But it would be facile to assume that Catalan opera buffs were ignorant merely because they were rich. By the 1880s a serious audience had formed around the Liceu. As the novelist-critic Eduardo Mendoza put it, its strong bias in musical issues sublimated political debate, so that "for several decades the opera, with all its emotional content, offered the Barcelonans a convenient, agreeable duelling-ground."

The Liceu was nominally a public place, at least for those who could pay for tickets—and it went without saying that no worker could. It had an attachment, however, the Club del Liceu, which one could enter directly from the upper floor and was entirely private, members only: the inner sanctum of privilege for box holders, their wives, their mistresses, and their friends. When the Liceu itself burned down in 1861 and again in 1994, the club survived the fires.

Today there is probably no spot in Barcelona that so preserves, as though in amber, the feeling of exclusivity which was part of the unspeakable joy of late nineteenth-century wealth. From its ground-floor entrance, sumptuously ornamented with stained-glass narratives illustrating climactic moments of Wagner's operas, to the highly decorated dining room, to the circular room containing a series of paintings illustrating boulevard life by the Barcelonan impressionist Ramón Casas—which feature an open touring car driving straight at you with its headlights ablaze with real forty-watt electricity and two pretty girls riding in it—the entire place is a masterful period piece, weirdly eclectic and perfectly preserved.

The first time I went there, almost forty years ago, I was taken by Xavier Corberó and, apart from two elderly Catalan gentlemen attired in tight suits and wing collars, we had the dining room to ourselves, and our dishes of *rap al all cremat* (monkfish with burnt garlic) and bright green peas with mint were served to us by waiters who looked older than the turtles of the Galápagos. Today this relative solitude would hardly be possible, because a later and younger generation of the rich have discovered the Club del Liceu and fill it to near bursting point every night, accompanied by girls of the *bones famílies* who, given a change of costume and maquillage, could just a moment ago have stepped out of a Casas painting. The waiting list for membership is years long, just as it used to be. In Barcelona, nothing old is out of date any more.

The Liceu was Barcelona's core image of high-bourgeois culture. But its programs did not sit well with all Catalan musicians. The problem was their content. The low emphasis put on purely orchestral work, the fixation on Italian opera and the disproportionate influence of private sponsors—all these were annoying. They reinforced the idea that the only "real" music came from abroad, a notion that true Catalanists found obnoxious. Moreover, the Liceu's policies seemed to imply that good, "cultivated" music belonged only to the rich. This snobbery collided with the ideologies of Catalanism and socialism, brewing at the edge of the Renaixenca, a conflict which came to a head over *cançó popular,* traditional Catalan folk music. The great supporter and defender of this musical form, who set off a grassroots revival of choral singing in Catalunya and whose work stimulated the Catalans to build one of their most extraordinary architectural masterpieces—far more important, as architecture, than the Liceu—was Josep Anselm Clavé i Camps (1824-1875).

Clavé was a musician, a song collector, and a socialist politician. His ideas about the role of music in society had been formed in the 1850s: initially, by a man named Abdo Terradas, a socialist agitator who preached that the democracy he wanted for Catalunya could only be reached through a broad class rising based on education, which would bring factory hands together with shopkeepers, artisans with intellectuals. Part of the key to this alliance would be musical literacy. Music, choral singing especially, brought people together. It helped men and women, Clavé argued, "who have been turned into mere laboring machines" to recover their damaged dignity and self-esteem through shared esthetic experience and cooperation. Choral societies, he said, would wean city workers away from the "sordid ambience" of their taverns, their drunken binges in search of oblivion. Self-improvement through musical education: It was not a joke, not something the nobs could condescend to. By the 1860s Clavé's nobly democratic influence had created workers' choral societies, known as the *cors de Clavé*, Clavé's choirs, all over Catalunya, for Catalans—especially the working class—loved voluntary association. He arranged their programs, recruited conductors, trained them, supplied them sheet music for old songs, and new ones as well.

Clavé's own compositions were very popular. "Els Flors de Maig—The Flowers of May" of 1859 was a perennial hit with Catalan choristers. He also wrote patriotic anthems, work songs, hymns to labor, and ditties in praise of folk culture and popular festivals. And he tried to carry on a career in electoral politics, though his efforts did not have any of the political effect of his musical work.

Some of the native voice, however, was not sung; it lived in recitation, or on the printed page. A bizarre instrument of cultural Catalanism was a poetry contest known as the Jocs Florals, or Floral Games. This competition was itself a revival of an older Catalan practice, which had fallen into disuse. Its object was to confirm that a great patriotic literature was being written in Catalan, which might stir Catalans into separatist fervor. To do this, it must be archaic in diction. As one Majorcan poet wrote in the 1850s:

Cec d'amor per un llenguatge,
que no tinc prou dominat
emprenc el pelerinatge
pel fossar del temps passat.

Blind with love for a language,
All too powerless today,
I set out on a pilgrimage
Through the graveyard of olden times.

The first poet to set out through the "graveyard" actually worked in a finance house in Madrid and, though unquestionably Catalan and much given to boasting piteously about the *enyorança* (nostalgic longing) he felt for his native soil, did not actually go so far as to live on it. His name was Bonaventura Carles Aribau i Farriols (1798-1862). He had dreams of becoming a Chateaubriand, a Byron, exhorting his fellow Catalans to regain their ancient liberties and, especially, the right to use their native tongue. To this end he wrote an ode, "La Pàtria—The Fatherland." It proved to be the work of art with which the Catalan Renaixença began. For there he was, supposedly pining away in Madrid, and realizing that his native language—*la llengua llemosina,* the Catalan tongue—lay at the heart of belonging. It contains all his recognizable images from birth onward. Only in Catalan can he think straight. "Let me speak again," he cries, in a transport of loss:

> *The tongue of those wise men*
> *who filled the world with their customs and laws,*
> *the tongue of the strong men who served the kings,*
> *defended their rights, avenged their insults.*
> *Beware, beware the ungrateful man whose lips utter*
> *his native accent in a far country and does not weep,*
> *who thinks of his origins without pangs of yearning,*
> *nor takes his fathers' lyre from the holy wall!*

For literate Catalans, resentful of the political dominance of Madrid, this was venturesome stuff. And even as a twentieth-century Australian, I found its moping and somewhat defensive tone—for the Catalans are quite capable of feeling those pangs of enyoranca without actually leaving their native soil—quite comprehensible, even familiar. Neither culture was fully self-sustaining: Aribau freely chose to work in Madrid, after all, whilst bemoaning his "exile," and continued to do so long after publishing "La Pàtria," even though he could presumably have worked in one of the other banks that flourished in Barcelona's energetic mercantile economy—and he felt a tad guilty about it, which led to poses of exaggerated independence and virtue. But despite his expatriate status, or perhaps even partly because of it, Aribau came to be seen as the founder of literary Catalanism, and his array of patriotic images would dominate the discourse of Catalan independence for the next half century, combining to form an idealized feudal past.

So every year, from 1859 on, a little elite of Catalans would gather in Barcelona to recite praises of Catalan virtue and Catalan history in terms so precious, stilted, and old-fashioned that few other people could understand them, even if they were Catalan. But their feelings about the need for Catalan as common speech as well as a literary medium were widely shared, for, as the arch-conservative bishop of Vic, Josep Torras i Bagès, wrote in *The Catalan Tradition,* "The word or the tongue of a people is the manifestation and glow of its substance, the image of its figure, and he who knows the language knows the people who speak it; once the tongue disappears, so do the people."

Until well into the 1880s the Jocs Florals were considered the "spinal column," as one writer put it, of the Renaixença; they were taken as the annual proof that the Catalan language was the main conduit of elevated national feeling. They were, in a sense, a medieval revival, though the original Jocs Florals—a troubadour's competition, in which poets competed for prizes from the court—do not seem to have been held often. They began, supposedly, in 1324, when seven young nobles met in Toulouse and decided to invite poets and troubadours from all over the *paisos catalans* to take part in a poetry competition, an *eisteddfod,* the next year.

By the early 1400s, the Jocs Florals were almost a tradition in Barcelona and they offered three trophies. The third prize was a violet made of silver. The second prize was a golden rose. But the first prize was a *flor natural,* a real rose. It would wither and die, of course, but it was a reminder that no work of art could rival nature. The prize would fade; the poem would last in the hearts of readers.

The Jocs Florals died in the Middle Ages and were soon a memory, not a living tradition. They were not revived until nearly 1860, by which time the practice of writing Catalan verse began to consolidate again.

But one should take care not to put the cart before the horse. Catalan was not preserved as a language by the mere fact that some poets wished to write in it, and made big efforts to do so. What guaranteed the integrity and continuity of Catalan was, quite simply, common speech. People just kept speaking it, despite the ridiculous and, finally, unpoliceable edicts against it from Madrid, whose purpose in forbidding the language was to destroy the sense of self that a bludgeoned people retained. People do not speak a language because patriotic poems are written in it, and they do not give up speaking it because those same poems are censored. They speak it, and keep speaking it, because they learned it long before they could read. In Aribau's words, "My first infant wail was in Catalan / when I sucked the sweet milk from my mother's nipple." If Catalan had not been spoken as the vernacular of the people of Barcelona and the rest of Catalunya, it would have perished, just as Latin usage perished, withering on the social vine. But it did not.

Catalan is a moderately difficult language for a foreigner to learn, but certainly no harder than Spanish or Italian, both of which, being descended from Latin, it closely resembles. Certainly it is not difficult in the acute way that Basque is. Nobody, including the Basques themselves, seems to have the foggiest notion where Basque comes from. It resembles no other tongue spoken on Earth; whereas Catalan's relation to Latin is clear and straightforward. It is the fruit of the Roman occupation, more than two thousand years ago.

But (to simplify a little) part of its peculiar character, its *fet differencial,* as one would call it in Catalan, is that it originates in a different kind of Latin, the "low" vernacular spoken by the Roman line soldiers rather than "high" literary Latin. That is why it has so many words in common with other Latin-rooted European languages. "Fear" in Catalan is *por,* in Italian, *paura,* in French, *peur,* and so on, all coming down from the Latin *pavor.* Whereas in Spanish it is *miedo,* reflecting the "high" Latin word for it, *metus.*

The official line given out by the Franco regime used to be that Catalan was a degenerate form of Spanish, a sort of hillbilly Spanish gone to seed, or at best a mere dialect. This has never been true. They are distinct tongues, each with its own linguistic integrity. If you measure the importance of a language by the literary works written in it, then it is obvious that Castilian Spanish comes out dominant. But what do you expect, when Catalan speakers are such a minority in Spain's general population? This does not imply a lack of Catalan masterpieces; some would say that the greatest early chivalric novel produced in Spain was itself a parody of the chivalric mode, an exceedingly funny and occasionally scabrous epic named *Tirant lo Blanc,* written in Catalan. But it is a novel more cited in academe than read with gusto in real life.

Not everyone in Barcelona speaks Catalan, and indeed for official purposes the definition of "Catalan" is not a linguistic one. There has been too much migration from other parts of Spain, notably Andalusia; and since everyone there speaks Spanish as a matter of course, those who arrive speaking *only* Spanish have only the weakest of incentives to learn and regularly use Catalan.

And so, when I tried out my few Catalan phrases, hoping to start at least the rudiments of a cat-sat-on-the-mat dialogue in this strange language, I failed utterly. If the person I addressed (behind the bar, say) was Catalan, he or she would reply in Spanish out of courtesy, to make things easier for the foraster. Or else he or she would answer in Spanish to make it plain that no foraster could possibly be expected to have grasped enough of the ancient, melodious, complex, and rich tongue of Catalunya to make any conversation in it worthwhile. Either way, one tended to be shut out.

THREE

IT IS A STRANGE FACT—WELL, IT CAN ALWAYS BE ARGUED ABOUT, but it seems a fact to me—that although Barcelona in the twenty-five years between 1885 and 1910 produced a flowering in architecture, not much of the kind happened in painting and sculpture.

Later it did foster two Catalan painters, who went on to make a great impact on world painting after 1920 and without whose work modern art, surrealism especially, would have been much impoverished: Salvador Dalí (1904-1989) and Joan Miró (1893-1983).

But in the last decades of the nineteenth century, the time Catalans always liked to call their Renaixenca, although there was expert, witty, and sometimes moving painting done in Barcelona in the studios of Ramón Casas, Santiago Rusinyol, and others, it did not add much to the substantial glories of fin-de-siècle European art, and could scarcely be compared to the achievements of the school of Paris. Barcelona fostered Picasso, but Picasso was not a Catalan artist, just passing through. Barcelona had no figure of comparable greatness to Adolf Menzel in Germany or Isaac Levitan in Russia, Frederic Church in the United States, or even (at his best) Arthur Streeton in Australia. In fact one of the things that struck me most forcibly about late nineteenth-century Catalan painting, when I first saw some examples of it in the Museu d'Art Modern in Barcelona back in the late 1960s, was how much it resembled the kind of impressionism that filled the museums of Sydney and Melbourne—the tonal impressionism, descending mainly from James McNeill Whistler, whose influence swept London, Paris, New York, and places as far apart as Melbourne and Mexico City, in the 1890s. One might have been looking at Tom Roberts and Arthur Streeton, with a grayer light and the gum trees edited out.

Catalunya's Renaixenca did not translate into English as "Renaissance." Catalunya never had a Renaissance, not in the Italian sense. What it did have was generally enjoyable but largely derivative painting and sculpture, and plenty of architecture of stunning and almost implausible originality.

Domènech i Montaner (1849-1923) was the great theorist, and the practical all-rounder as well, of Catalan architectural nationalism. He was widely traveled, deeply read, and a scholar of everything from iron forging to medieval heraldry. The son of a Barcelonan bookbinder, he was a protean figure: a gifted draftsman, a historian with a solid base in fieldwork, a nationalist politician, an inspiring teacher, and a publisher who turned his father's firm, Editorial Montaner i Simón, into Spain's leading creator of *éditions de luxe.* Though he was more politically conservative than William Morris in England, he was a somewhat analogous figure and as delightfully attractive a personality.

He was absorbed by the enormous problem of defining the parameters of a national architecture. All talk about design and building, he claimed in a manifesto published in 1878, has to center on this. In writing, we can say who we are. We can imagine painting that makes similar declarations. And so can music. But can architecture do it? And if so, how? On what terms of material and style? In his manifesto Domènech laid the foundations (at least in theory) for an architecture which could be genuinely and forthrightly modern while still incorporating regional difference.

As Europeans living at the end of the nineteenth century, he argued, we all live in a culture which is still, in some sense, a museum. Thanks to the multiplication of images through publication and reproduction, we can get access to a huge vocabulary of prototype and shape. We can copy Greek, Gothic, Vitruvian, Indian, Egyptian, and Islamic building forms, and it behooves us to be proficient in all of them. But none of these attach to our central myth. This myth is nothing other than Technology. In a world of iron, glass, chemistry, and electricity, Domènech wrote, "mechanical science determines the rudiments of architectural form" and "everything heralds the appearance of a new era for architecture."

The demands of architecture, he went on, go far beyond the merely scholarly. Spain has two great wells of architecture. One is the Romanesque and Gothic in Catalunya, especially in Barcelona. The other, in the south, is Islamic: Granada, Seville, Córdoba. Neither excludes the other and local patriotism must not make it seem to. A truly national architecture, said Domènech, has to draw strength from them and use them, but it will not come into being from merely copying them. "Only societies without firm, fixed ideas," he wrote, "which fluctuate between today's thinking and yesterday's, without faith in tomorrow—only these societies fail to inscribe their histories in durable monuments." And, if you think of American postmodernism a century later, with its flittering clever references to architectural style, how right he was!

Domènech quoted too, and incessantly. But he did so with intelligence and verve. He was only thirty-seven when he was asked to do two of the main buildings of the 1888 Universal Exposition in Barcelona. The Café-Restaurant survives and is a landmark in modernista design. The Hotel Internacional was demolished after the fair, but from what we know of it Domènech was already, at this tender age for an architect, a master of building systems. Barcelona then had no hotels that even the most fervent Catalan patriot would have called first rate (and as a matter of fact, it still overrates its own hotels in the guidebooks). But he brought off the feat, incredible by modern standards of construction management, of finishing the Hotel Internacional, a five-story iron-frame structure clad in brick and terra-cotta, with 1,600 rooms and street elevations five hundred feet long, within budget and on time. We have no idea how well it would have stood up to the wear and tear of long-term use, but merely to finish it was a phenomenal feat of organization.

The Café-Restaurant, however, is with us yet in its changed incarnation as a zoological museum. It looks medieval, with its crenellations and white ceramic shields. Some of these shields, however, are a prediction of pop art—instead of armorial bearings, they carry advertising slogans for Catalan produce, such as the drinks the Café-Restaurant was offering its clients, and are a light-hearted parody of Domènech's own interest in heraldic history.

But the building is made of plain brick and industrial iron. The span between its medievalism and the modernity of its materials is what makes the Café-Restaurant an early modernista landmark.

To use plain brick in 1888 was considered close to a violation of etiquette. Brick was a "dumb" material. The very word for brick in Catalan, *totxo,* means "ugly, stupid." The notion of making a *festive* building from brick was unheard of in Catalunya.

But Domènech thought brick ought to be used plainly. You could make practically any shape you wanted from it: flat Catalan arches, round Moorish ones, cogging, diapers, tricky reveals, corbels. Being made from the very earth of the homeland, brick was patriotic. It was *clar i català,* in a phrase used by both him and his younger colleague Puig i Cadafalch, and by Gaudí, too—clear and Catalan. The same with iron, about whose unembellished use young Domènech was just as explicit. He let his iron beams show, and no effort was made to dissemble the iron window frames and door jambs of the Café-Restaurant. He used painted, glazed, and molded ornament, but never to deny the structure underneath—a habit of mind that reached an extreme in the thick blossoming of ceramic and mosaic roses across the structural grid of his Palau de la Música, 1905-08.

The Palau de la Música, and his enormous Hospital de la Santa Creu i Sant Pau (finished two years later), are the masterworks of Domènech's long, varied career. Both show his genius for innovative planning. In doing the hospital he was expected to work within the square grid of Cerdà's Eixample, but the project was so large—a site of nine full city blocks—that he didn't feel obliged to.

Barcelona in 1900 had never had an acceptable hospital. In the Raval, next to the Ramblas, the Hospital de la Sant Creu (Holy Cross) dated from the fifteenth century. Luckily for the Barcelonans, it was ruined in a fire in 1887. A new hospital had to be built. It made sense to erect it in the Eixample, on the less traffic-heavy and crowded side of town. After some dickering among the trustees, the job went to Domènech's office.

An enormous site was allotted—360 acres of urban space. Cleared and excavated, it would produce a garden city skewed at forty-five degrees to the grid city, since, Domènech declared, he loathed "the eternal monotony of two widely separated parallel lines." Then this site would become one enormous basement, holding all the

Domènech's Hospital de la Santa Creu i Sant Pau

service areas of the hospital: operating theaters, storage, circulation, machinery—all underground. Above, at ground level, set among gardens, would be the richly decorated entrance block and the forty-eight pavilions for staff and patients.

The Hospital de Sant Pau, then, was not a mere building but a large controlled environment. Keeping up the patients' mood was a necessary part of the control. To lift their spirits and banish some of the association of hospitals with death and suffering, Domènech lavished his imagination on the detail of each building.

The facade sparkles with mosaics depicting the history of hospitals back to the Middle Ages. Octagonal columns support shallow domes, and the whole vestibule is bathed in golden light from a stained-glass *claraboia,* or skylight, in the roof. Domènech, like Henri Matisse, believed that color had an actual therapeutic effect. It made you want to recover and live. His son recalled that "the material took on nobility even if it was ordinary ... [In] the Hospital of Sant Pau, ... he thought that everything that could give a feeling of well-being to the sick was also a form of therapy." With inventive brio Domènech designed the effervescent roof-scape of pavilion domes, and the profusion of sculpture—allegorical, historical, or just decorative—that everywhere greets the visitor's eye. He gave the sculpture program to two masters, Eusebi Arnau and Pau Gargallo, who in turn employed dozens of assistant carvers and ceramists.

Oddly enough, there are no references to the Hospital de Sant Pau in English travel writing of the day. Yet perhaps it is not so odd, since passing Anglo-American eyes, used to the punitive grimness of their own hospitals at the time, might not even have identified this marvelous complex as being a hospital at all.

The quintessential building of Domènech's career, however, was the Palau de la Música Catalana. It was the one real institution of modernist culture that rose in Barcelona in the 1890s, prospered thereafter, and continues undiminished today. It housed a choral society, the Orfeó Català, which had been created to carry forward the work of Josep Clavé, father of Catalunya's folk-music revival in the 1860s. The Orfeó was started by two young men, neither of whom had ever met Clavé, but they both adored him and his work. Both were obsessed by cançó popular.

They would expand Clavé's work by using folk music as the ordinary public's bridge to *música universal,* classical music. Their choral society and its *Orfeonistes* would mingle folk music with symphonic and choral works by Bach, Beethoven, Handel, Wagner, Haydn, Berlioz, and Mahler.

Especially, there would be Wagner. Clavé had been mad for Wagner, but it was not a generally shared enthusiasm in Barcelona back in the 1860s. However, this changed by 1870, and now musical Catalanists saw the future, as one of them put it, in "Wagnerism, considered as an instrument and a sign of national culture."

Why did Catalanists make such a cult of Wagner? Because they saw in his work for Germany an achieved parallel to their own desire to create a myth of national identity for Catalunya. Wagner's heroes had been to Catalunya. Their holy mountains were his holy mountains. "My name is Parsifal, and I come from Montsalvat"—Catalunya *was* Wagnerian Spain.

And there was a more general reason. The antiquity of Wagner's themes contrasted with the daring modernity of his musical forms. This fit perfectly with the spirit of the Catalan Renaixenca that now suffused the city's most advanced architecture. Wagner had intended the *Ring* cycle to be the founding epic of Bavaria, as Virgil's *Aeneid* was of Rome. Its mission was to describe the identity of the German race. Likewise, the Renaixenca was focused on, obsessed by, the supposed uniqueness of the Catalan race. It wanted to find its "modernism" by evoking an idealized past, albeit an absolutely mythic one.

No wonder then that Catalanists saw Wagner's operas as a guide to combining myths of a legendary past with the overarching myth of progress and innovation. Germany, too, was a culture identified with yearning and unattained idealism—enyoranca, as Catalan put it. Wagner's vision of the "total work of art," in which all media played a part, had a strong allure for architects who were working out of a deep craft base and sought to combine the talents of painters, ceramists, bronze casters, iron smiths, joiners, glaziers, mosaicists, and masons. All these are represented at an abnormally rich level of skill and display in the Palau de la Música Catalana, the most Wagnerian building in Barcelona— or the world.

Detail of exterior, Palau de la Música Catalana

Whenever I visit the palau it amazes me: One never gets used to Domènech's invention and daring. Perhaps no architect has ever used color more subtly or riskily than this Catalan. His building is actually quite small:

The site is only fifteen thousand square feet, a fraction of the Liceu's. So there was not the space to amaze a public with sweeping architectonic effects. Color would do it instead. The foyer, its shallow vaults sheathed in pale ocher and aquamarine embossed tiles, and the staircase, with its squat golden-glass balusters, prepares you to enter the auditorium.

You will not be disappointed. The concert hall of the palau is a large box of pink stained glass. From the middle of its ceiling a huge and spectacular claraboia swells down, like an inverted bell or a pendulous breast. Its motif is a circle of angelic choristers, diffusing a soft pink-and-blue radiance from high up.

Domènech's effort to dematerialize the structure of the palau even extends to the chandeliers that hang around the main columns of the auditorium without seeming to touch them, looking like colossal Byzantine earrings. Domènech has taken Gothic stone and glass and transposed it into steel and glass, making a perfectly explicit link between the ancient and the new. The main loads of the palau's auditorium are carried on a steel frame, so that it becomes a glass box permeated by daylight. The decorative advantages of this arrangement are spectacular. The practical disadvantages of it were also large: Josep Pla, Barcelona's essayist, complained with some asperity about trying to listen to Chopin against the background racket of brewers' delivery carts rumbling over the cobblestones outside. The palau is a true curtain-wall building, one of the first in the world, and this is hardly to its advantage as a performance space. It has all the acoustic problems of that idiom.

When finished, the palau cost nearly twice its intended budget (875,000 pesetas against 475,000). There was some criticism of this from the habitually frugal Catalans, who complained that the project lacked what they considered their national virtue—seny, or common sense. But to enter it today is to realize that it would have been cheap at five times the cost, especially after the brilliant restoration carried out in the 1990s by the architect Oscar Tusquets.

As if the decorative flamboyance of the palau weren't enough, it was also given a complicated sculpture pro-gram. It tells stories, and implies cultural affinities in some detail, following out Clavé's belief in the continuity between popular and universal music, local and trans-national cultures. On the facade, for instance, música universal is symbolized by busts of Palestrina, Bach, Beethoven, and—who else?—Wagner. On one ground-floor corner, which juts into the street like a stone prow, is an allegory of Catalan folk song dominated by a figure of one of the rebellious seventeenth-century *segadors,* with his reaping hook and beret.

The palau's most spectacular sculpture, however, is reserved for the concert hall. This object, or perhaps "manifesto" would be a better word for it, is the proscenium, designed by Domènech to follow an idea by Lluís Millet. At first sight it is quite jarring, apparently made of white plaster (actually, a soft white pumice) which looks ghostly and weird against the solid riot of color from the hall's ceramic and glasswork.

On the left side, the proscenium arch depicts cançó popular, songs of the people. It bears a bust of Josep Anselm Clavé with a willow tree rising beside him. A garland of flowers is being plaited from his pedestal by an art nouveau maiden with flowing hair; another, below, gathers blossoms. The subject is a famous song written by Clavé, "Els Flors de Maig—The Flowers of May"):

> *Under a pollarded willow, a girl*
> *joyously plaits her rich golden hair;*
> *her gaze is a cool crystal fountain*
> *wood-violets adorn her....*

On the opposite side of the proscenium, música universal is personified by a bust of Beethoven, between two Doric columns. (Doric, the order of the Parthenon, was considered the classical emblem par excellence, plain and masculine. Beethoven was taken by Catalans to be a classical, not a Romantic, composer. This view of him also obtained in his native Germany.) He is significantly lower than Clavé, who seems to be gazing over his head.

Above that head, new music is being born. A rolling cloud of stone vapor, suggesting inspiration, starts between the Doric columns and boils upward—to morph into Wagner's Valkyries on their winged steeds. They thunder silently across the top of the proscenium arch, toward Clavé and his willow tree—the inventiveness of new foreign music reaching toward the (literal) roots of old Catalan culture.

Singers and orchestra are framed in this huge white metaphor as a permanent reminder of the Orfeó's original purpose. Full color then resumes on the back wall of the stage, a hemicycle designed by the ceramist Eusebi Arnau, which forms a permanent background to the changing musical programs. It is made of *trencadis,* broken tiles, from which grow eighteen three-dimensional maidens playing eighteen instruments, from flute to zither. Their bodies from the waist down are flat with the wall and linked to one another by swooping garlands. But their heads and upper bodies, as well as their instruments, are modeled in the round.

No modernista building in Barcelona was or ever would be as ecstatically received as Domènech's Palau de la Música Catalana. It was, said the jury that gave it the Ajuntament's prize for the best building of 1908, a demonstration of the "genius and art characteristic of Catalunya, strong as its race, great as its history and beautiful as its incomparable sky." Naturally, as the critical fortunes of modernisme went into decline twenty years on, so did the palau's reputation. Soon its neighbors would be calling it the Palau de la Quincalleria Catalana, the Palace of Catalan Junk. There was always complaint about its acoustical properties which, since the palau was essentially a glass box, were always faulty. Some talked of demolishing it. But the palau has never gone into eclipse and now, thankfully, it never will. What saved it from oblivion—apart from the architecture itself, in all its aggressive memorability—was its role as a nursery of musical talent and a condenser of Catalan patriotism. There probably isn't a musician alive who, having had the luck to perform in the palau, hasn't felt like complaining about its faults, not to mention those of the Orfeó Català itself. But it seems to enshrine the very heart of Catalan musical culture, and apart from Carnegie Hall there is no other musical institution in the world that evokes such intense, even furious, loyalties from great performers. Pau Casals was devoted to the place; the seven-year-old Alicia de Larrocha made her debut there in 1929; and I have never forgotten the sight of Montserrat Caballe striking her imposing bosom with an almost audible thump and declaiming, in the course of an interview we did on stage, that "tomorrow night I shall sing in *my* palau." The palau's management could be a tad conservative but it always caught up with advanced musical taste in the end, and it is the only cultural institution (there being none in the sister fields of literature or the visual arts) that managed to remain both Catalanist and international, and for more than a century at that, thus showing that a strong regional culture is not fated to be provincial, in Barcelona or elsewhere.

THE MOST FAMOUS ARCHITECT—INDEED, FOR MANY PEOPLE today, especially foreign visitors, the single most famous human being—that Barcelona ever produced was killed by a streetcar one June day in 1926, as he toddled across Gran Via near the corner of Carrer Bailen. Evidently he was lost in thought and fairly deaf, so that he neither saw the No. 30 tram bearing down on him nor heard the passersby shouting their warnings. He was an old codger in a rusty black suit. His pockets were empty (except, by one account, for some orange peel), he carried

The Sagrada Família in the 1920s

neither identification nor money, and he was taken at first for one of the thousands of seedy old pensioners with whom the city abounded. Only later, as he lay dying in the public hospital, was it found that he was the seventy-four-year-old Antoni Gaudí, architect of the unfinished temple of the Sagrada Família and a dozen other smaller (but, many believe, better) buildings in and just outside his city.

The Sagrada Família, or, to give its full name, the Templo de la Sagrada Família (Expiatory Temple of the Holy Family), is beyond rival the best-known structure in Catalunya. It is to Barcelona what the Eiffel Tower is to Paris or the Harbour Bridge to Sydney: a completely irreplaceable logo. Being unfinished, it is also much misunderstood, starting with the fact that so many of the millions of tourists who visit it every year imagine that it is a "cathedral." But Barcelona had already had a perfectly fine cathedral since feudal times. The Sagrada Família was intended to be what its name says: a "temple," where Catalans (and, Gaudí hoped, eventually the whole Catholic world) would converge to do penance for the sins of "modernity," sins which had so horribly and mortally offended Christ, his Virgin Mother, and—presumably when he wasn't busy carpentering—Christ's stepfather, St. Joseph. Viewed in the context of Church history, this made sense, admittedly of a somewhat lugubrious kind. In the last third of the nineteenth century, the Catholic Church felt it was under siege from all those forces of atheism, scientism, disobedience, and doubt, which its hierarchy rolled together into the portmanteau word, modernism. Because of this, massive rearguard actions were fought by Rome. There was Pope Pius IX's "Syllabus of Errors," launched against the threat of a growing liberalism and listing just about every conceivable advanced or critical idea about sin, belief, and duty as a loathsome heresy, to be punished in hellfire. Extreme dogmas were promulgated, such as that of papal infallibility. It is probably true to say that between 1830 and the death of the ultraconservative Pope Pius IX in 1878, the Catholic Church became more ferocious in its perception of heretical threat than it had been since the time of the Crusades. It could no longer burn the actual bodies of sinners, but it certainly could and did cut them off from the body of the Church and participation in the Sacraments, and threaten them with eternal punishment in the afterlife. And Gaudí, to whom a penitential relationship with an implacable God was the very core of religious belief, was just the architect to convey this in stone. What the Church wanted was a new Counter-Reformation, based on an extreme ratcheting-up of cultic devotion to Jesus, Mary, and the saints. Gaudí conceived his temple as a means to that end. It would be an ecstatically repressive building that would help atone for the "excesses" of democracy: Not only was Gaudí more Catholic than the pope, he was more royalist than the king, not that he thought the king was worth much compared to the pope. Anyone so misdirected as to imagine that radicalism in art is in some necessary way connected to radicalism in politics, and that its purpose is to make men happy, might think about Gaudí and be corrected. "Everyone has to suffer," he once told a disciple. "The only ones who don't suffer are the dead. He who wants an end to suffering wants to die."

Gaudí was born in 1852 in Reus, a fair-size provincial town in the Baix Camp (lower plains) of Tarragona. He came from an artisan family of metalsmiths who had married into the families of other smiths, for generations back. Their workshop near Reus was known as the Mas de la Caldera, or "caldronmaker's house."

The country around Tarragona, when Gaudí was a boy, had changed little since it was parceled out to Roman settlers nearly two millennia before. Gaudí developed a passionate curiosity about its plants, animals, and geology. Nature, he said later, was the "Great Book, always open, that we should force ourselves to read." Everything structural or ornamental was already prefigured in natural form, in limestone grottoes, a beetle's shining wing case, or the twisty corrugations of an ancient olive trunk.

Gaudí never ceased to draw on, and from, nature. Each paving block of Passeig de Gràcia features a starfish and an octopus, originally designed for the Casa Batlló. Turtles and tortoises support the columns of the Nativity facade of the Sagrada Família, which also has thirty different species of stone plants copied from the vegetation of Catalunya and the Holy Land. Mushrooms become domes, or columns with capitals. The columns of the Güell Crypt are a grove of brick trunks, sending out branches—the ribbed vaults—that lace into one another.

Gaudí knew and never forgot country building in stone, clay, and timber—materials (he said, with a sovereign disregard for the leisure hours of common folk, which he expected them to sacrifice willingly for the greater glory of God and perhaps of Gaudí, too) that "can be gathered by the peasants themselves in their spare time between their labors." Thus the rough stone walls of terraces in the Baix Camp became the "rustic" colonnades of the Güell Park. In the latter years of his life, when making the figures for the Nativity facade of the Sagrada Família, he made literal transcriptions from nature by chloroforming birds and even a donkey so as to cast them in plaster. Sometimes this effigy-making was of a rather more gruesome kind: Since nobody, and certainly not the bristly and childless patriarch Gaudí, could induce a live baby to be still, when he needed infants for his scene of the "Slaughter of the Innocents" on the Nativity facade he got permission from the nuns in the old Hospital de la Sant Creu to cast the corpses of stillborn babies in plaster. There exists an old photo of one of Gaudí's studios, looking like a charnel house or perhaps the dreadful ogre's cave of Polyphemus in *The Odyssey,* with plaster limbs and bodies hanging on every wall.

But what mattered most to Gaudí was twofold. First, the forms and structural principles that could be deduced from inanimate matter, such as plants. And second, his own artisan background.

This ancestry mattered immensely to the architect. He thought of himself, not as a theoretician, but as a man of his hands. He said, no doubt truthfully, that he learned about complex curvatures and membrane structures by watching his father beat iron and copper sheets, making up the forms without drawing them first, producing the miracle of volume and enclosure from the banality of flatness. It is a fact that tells you almost all you need to know about why Gaudí was not a "modern" architect, in the Mies-Gropius-Le Corbusier sense of "modernity." Unlike such people, unlike even his Catalan contemporaries Domènech i

Montaner and Puig i Cadafalch, he thought in terms of manual not conceptual space. Others were ruled by the grid; Gaudí didn't give beans for it. His mature work cannot even be imagined adequately from flat drawings. Its surfaces twist and wiggle. The space flares, solemnly inflates, then collapses again. Gaudí did not like to draw; drawing did not preserve enough information about the complex volumes and hollows he carried in his head. He much preferred to make models, from wood, paper, clay, or cut turnips.

Gaudí's instinctive preference for the haptic over the conceptual worked against him when he entered the school of architecture, housed in the Llotja in Barcelona, where he would study from 1873 to 1877. Because abstractions bored him and he did not think easily in terms of orthographic projection (T-square architecture: plan, elevation, section), he did poorly as a student—not the first time that a genius at school has seemed not to be one. His teachers were far more interested in transmitting the basics of Greco-Roman planning and ornament than in teaching what most interested Gaudí, rural vernacular building ("architecture without architects") and Catalan medievalism. Both fused, or so he came to believe, in a unique sensibility which was nationalist at root and could only be expressed in Catalunya. "Our strength and superiority lies in the balance of feeling and logic," he wrote, "whereas the Nordic races become obsessive and smother feeling. And those of the South, blinded by the excess of color, abandon reason and produce monsters." This, though untrue, reveals not only Gaudí's regionalist mind-set but also, in its last five words, his acquaintance with Goya's "Caprichos."

One medieval complex in particular fired Gaudí's imagination as a teenager, and that of his close friend Eduardo Toda i Güell. It was the monastery of Santa Maria del Poblet, in the Baix Camp of Tarragona, within easy reach of Reus. This once mighty Cistercian foundation had begun in the mid-twelfth century and had benefited greatly from the church building boom that also trans-formed Barcelona itself in the fourteenth, during the reign of Peter the Ceremonious. Beginning with this monarch, all the kings of Aragon and Catalunya had been buried there. Hence, it was the national pantheon and its import, both historic and patriotic, was immense. As architecture it was the grandest Cistercian building in Catalunya, strong, severe, and plain. Its chapter house, nine vaulted square bays carried on four central columns, ranked with Santa Maria del Mar and the Saló del Tinell as one of the supreme formal utterances of early Catalan Gothic.

But when Gaudí and Toda were boys, Poblet was a ruin and they conceived the mad, devout notion of restoring it to at least a memory, an eloquent vestige of its former glories. To them it was an archsymbol of Catholic supremacy and Catalan identity, and the liberals had ruined it in the name of freedom and rights. "What is this freedom?" young Toda demanded in an angry verse, if it meant

> to rip up the tomb-slabs
> and violate the sepulchres of heroes
> and sow terror and death everywhere ...
> and smash monuments to rubble ...
> if this is freedom, a curse on it!

Thus in Gaudí's mind, religious conservatism—the more extreme, the nobler—fused with the retention of Catalan identity. The Mendizábal Laws, having forced the Church to sell its property, had condemned Poblet to desertion and decay. Gaudí obviously could not undertake its restoration on his own. Patrons must be found. And he had to have his own career as an architect. In the end, no private person offered to pay for the renewal of Poblet, but Gaudí did find a patron for his own work—the sort of patron artists dream of, one who shares all their creative obsessions and does not question their cost. He was Eusebi Güell i Bacigalupi, industrialist, rising politician, and quintessential grandee of the Catalan establishment.

Gaudí's first projects for Güell were a palace in Barcelona and a *finca,* a country estate, up the hill from Barcelona toward the medieval convent of Pedralbes. Of the Finca Güell, only the main gate and its flanking lodges were done to Gaudí's design. But the gate (1884) is an amazing work, a huge guardian dragon in wrought iron, illustrating a poem by the laureate of Catalan religious verse, Jacint Verdaguer.

The palace, which stands on Carrer Nou de la Rambla, is entirely Gaudí's. With it, his maturity as an artist really begins, and it is the first of his buildings to justify his posthumous fame. It was his showpiece and he took infinite pains over its design, doing at least three complete versions of its facade before settling on the final one. Everything from the parabolic entrance to the wooden louvers that sheathe the tribune on its rear facade in a curved membrane like the scales of an armadillo bears the mark of an insatiable inventiveness.

It is also intensely theatrical, which adapts it well to its present-day function as the library of the Institut del Teatre, the Theatrical Archive of Barcelona. This first emerges in the basement, where Güell stabled his horses and kept his carriages. Its rugged vaults spring from squat, fat, brick columns whose capitals are funguslike pads of cooked earth: a cavelike, Wagnerian crypt.

From the start, Gaudí and Güell shared a taste for morbid penitential rhetoric. It would be refined and developed as time passed. Sometimes it produced a gloomy mélange. But at other times, when brought under strict control, the result was a masterpiece, as in the columns and capitals that support the screens of the miradors in Palau Güell. Cut and polished from the metallic gray limestone of Garraf, a quarry that belonged to the Güell enterprises, they look as radically new as Brancusi's sculpture (which Gaudí, of course, had never seen). Their fairing and subtle concavities, their utter purity of line, seem to owe nothing to other sources, though they were possibly inspired by the thirteenth-century capitals in the refectory of Poblet.

The other unique aspect of Palau Güell is its roof: It is truly a masterpiece, a beautiful acropolis of chimneys and ventilators, dominated by a central spire which contains the high slender dome of the main salon.

There are twenty chimneys, all roughly similar in shape: an obelisk or cone mounted on a shaft, which sits on a base, the whole sheathed in fragments of tile or glass. This kind of tilework is ancient and predates Gaudí, although many foreigners wrongly suppose that he invented it. It is known as *trencadis, trencar* being the Catalan verb "to break." It originated with the Arabs in Spain, but Gaudí was the first architect to revive it. It can cover curved surfaces, and it's cheap, too, because the material can be scrap. Gaudí was fascinated by how the mosaic fragmentation of trencadis, its shifts of color and pattern, could play against the solidity of architectural form, dissolving its stability. It is at least plausible that trencadis lies at the root of cubism, because the young Picasso, living just down the Carrer Nou de la Rambla from Palau Güell, would have seen its chimneys any day of the week. They are a prelude to the trencadis-covered serpentine benches in the Parc Güell, which Gaudí and his brilliant but lesser known colleague Josep Marià Jujol created as part of a large (but financially unsuccessful) housing project on Mont Pelat above Barcelona.

As an enlightened capitalist, Güell knew it was in his interest to reduce friction between workers and management. He thought this could be done by paternalism, avoiding the hard-fisted control that had caused riots, strikes, and machine breaking in other Barcelonan firms. So he decided to set up a self-contained *colonia,* or industrial village, for making cotton goods, velvet, and corduroy, south of Barcelona on the banks of the Llobregat River. Its workers would be isolated from the temptations of the big city. They could live, work, and pray together under the eye of the benign boss. All their needs would be taken care of. The Colonia Güell, as it was known, would have its own clinic and infirmary, its library, even a football club. Of course it would also have a church, which Gaudí would design.

Gaudí started thinking about the church in 1898 and the first stone was laid in 1908. When Eusebi Güell died ten years after that, the crypt was still unfinished and the church's walls above ground were scarcely underway. A few of Gaudí's surviving sketches show a monster edifice with parabolic spires that would have looked quite out of place in the Catalan countryside, though one can well imagine Gaudí replying that medieval cathedrals would have looked incongruous in the flat acres of northern France at first. But though it is only a fragment of a dream, the crypt of the Colonia Güell's church is one of Gaudí's masterworks, a building that looks wildly and arbitrarily expressive until one grasps the logic of construction that removes it from the domain of mere fantasy and creates one of Europe's greatest architectural spaces.

He did this upside down, with string and little bags of bird shot. Drawing out the ground plan of the crypt, he hung a string from each point where a column would meet the floor. Next he joined the hanging strings with cross-strings to simulate arches, beams, and vaults, attaching to each string a tiny bag of bird shot, its weight carefully scaled at so many milligrams per pellet to mimic the compressive load at each point. None of the strings in these complicated cat's cradles hung vertically. All the stresses in them were pure tension—the only way that string, which has zero resistance to bending, "knows" how to hang.

Gaudí then photographed the string model from all angles (seventy-two photographs, representing the rotation of the model five degrees at a time, totaling 360 degrees or one complete turn)—*and turned the photos upside down.*

Tension became compression and these "funicular" models (string models, in plain English, from the Latin *funis,* a cord) gave Gaudí a visual basis for making advanced and painstaking transferences. He could design forms without structural steel reinforcement that traditional masons could build in a brick-stone technology, which had not changed since the fourteenth century, when the wide shallow choir arch of Santa Maria del Pi was built. Gaudí wanted to imagine a kind of space that was both new and deeply archaic. The columns that support the roof of the crypt are hexagonal "pipes" of basalt, brought from a quarry in northern Catalunya and set in lead instead of mortar. (This gives the joints an imperceptible but sufficient flexibility under stress, whereas mortar would crumble.) They lean in a way that recalls ancient forms of shelter: the cave, the ledge, the hollow trunk. One of Gaudí's contemporaries, a friend of Josep

Pla named Rafael Puget, called Gaudí "not an architect of houses, but an architect of grottoes; not an architect of temples, but an architect of forests." It seemed so in the 1920s and still does today, and if you feel the crypt of the Colonia Güell is the great prototype of the far later, computer-designed structures by Frank Gehry, you are certainly right.

Josep Jujol's finest collaboration with Gaudí, apart from the Parc Güell, was done for another textile mogul: Josep Batlló i Casanovas. The Casa Batlló, on Passeig de Gràcia, was not done from scratch. It was a drastic conversion (1904-1906) of an existing apartment building from the late 1870s. By the time Gaudí was through with it, little survived of the original except the floor levels, and not all of those either. Jujol and Gaudí produced a new facade, an undulant sheet of mosaic wrapping around the windows (whose framing columns resemble bones)—a five-story crust of shifting, aqueous color which resembles nothing so much as one of Claude Monet's "Nymphéas," those enormous, shimmering paintings of light on water. It is one of the most exquisite sights in Spain, this jewel-box fantasy of a street wall surmounted by a roof made of what seem to be giant ceramic scales—which they are. The facade of Casa Batlló was meant to be read as an homage to Sant Jordi, patron of Barcelona. The

Casa Batlló

scales belong to the dragon he killed, as does the serpentine hump in the roof. The white balconies, pierced
with holes for eye sockets, are the skulls of the horrid
reptile's victims. The half-round tower set in the
facade ends in a form like a garlic bulb (Catalans, one
should remember, can never get enough garlic) surmounted by a cross. This is St. George's lance, and its
tip is inscribed with the holy and efficacious names of
Jesus, Mary, and Joseph.

When it was finished in 1906 the Casa Batlló became
the wonder of Passeig de Gràcia, and this distinction

invited competition. It came from the other side of the street, a few blocks uphill, where one of Batlló's friends, a property developer named Pere Milà i Camps, commissioned a new building from Gaudí. The Casa Milà, as it was called, was designed from the ground up, not adapted from an existing building. Its owner gave the architect a free hand. (By then it was clearly pointless *not* to give Gaudí complete design autonomy; without it, he would not consider a commission.)

He produced a sea cliff with caves in it for people. Its forged iron balconies are based on kelp and coral incrustation. Though La Pedrera ("the stone quarry," as Casa Milà was soon christened) looks formidably solid, with its massive projections and overhangs like the eye sockets of a Cyclopean head, it is much less so than it looks. The mighty folds and trunks of stone are actually more like stage grottoes. Despite its dramatic plasticity the stone is a skin and not, like true masonry, self-supporting.

Thus the Casa Milà becomes a kind of hermaphroditic fortress: on one hand, its maternal aspect—soft swelling, shelter, undulation; on the other the bizarre and contradictory "guardians" on the roof, invisible from the street. These are intensely masculine, so much so that George Lucas's costume designers based the figures of Darth Vader and the Death Star's guards on

Rooftop of Gaudí's Casa Milà

them—air-breathing and smoke-bearing totems, helmeted centurions which serve as chimneys and ventilators for the apartments below.

Singular though it is, La Pedrera fell short of Gaudí's original idea, a fact in which we are entitled to rejoice. Discussing Gaudí's taste, an acquaintance of his once remarked, was like talking about the "taste" of whales, something enormous, remote, and, in the end, meaningless. In some areas, like painting, he seems to have had no taste at all: The most beautiful color effects on Gaudían buildings usually turn out to be the work of Jujol, and the paintings Gaudí favored were usually repulsive in their gloomy, saccharine piety.

The same was true of his use of sculpture. It seems
almost beyond understanding that a man who created
some of the most marvelous three-dimensional forms of
his time—for no other words will do for the chimneys
of Palau Güell or the unfinished roof of Casa Milà—
could have wanted to add to his work the sort of vul-
garities Gaudí sometimes had in mind. A striking
example was the sculptural allegory of the holy rosary
(Rosario being the name of Milà's wife) that he planned
to put on top of the Casa Milà as its crowning feature,
culminating in a figure of the Virgin Mary flanked by
the archangels Gabriel and Michael, forty feet high and
in bronze—the Virgin as colossus. The artist Gaudí

wanted to do it was Carles Mani i Roig, whose vulgarity was as depressing as his piety was unassailable. The piety, it seems, counted most for Gaudí; in this respect the ugly sculptures being put on the Sagrada Família by its present anti-genius, Josep Subirachs, are desolatingly true to the Gaudían spirit. Mani i Roig would have turned La Pedrera into little more than a convoluted base for a huge, and hugely bad, sculpture. Perhaps its origins in Gaudí's imagination lay in another banal dominatrix of the skyline, the Statue of Liberty in New York Harbor.

That this did not happen was one of the few good results that can be attributed to the frenzy of church burning and street violence known as the Setmana Tragica or Tragic Week, which broke out in Barcelona in 1909 and came close to devastating the city. It was sparked by workers' resentment over a Spanish colonial war, which quickly devolved into a frenzy of anticlerical violence. This, a worse repeat of the Burning of the Convents in 1835, resulted in the destruction of some eighty churches, convents, and religious schools. Any building that declared itself to be Catholic was a potential target of popular wrath, and Milà sensibly figured that an apartment block with a giant Virgin Mary on its roof was unlikely to escape intact. So the commission, mercifully, never went ahead.

By now Gaudí had only one job left, the Sagrada Família. He had to raise the money for it; more or less alone, he had to keep its momentum going without any secure employer (one has to remember that the thing was not and never had been an official Church project). It was the obsession of his last years. In the wake of the Tragic Week it also became Barcelona's chief symbol of rebirth and transcendence for Gaudí's friend, the poet Joan Maragall:

> *Like a giant flower, a temple blossoms,*
> *amazing to be born here*
> *amid such a coarse and wicked people*
> *who laugh at it, blaspheme, brawl, vent their scorn*
> *against everything human and divine.*
> *Yet among misery, madness and smoke*
> *the temple (so precious!) rises and flourishes,*
> *waiting for the faithful who must come.*

The Expiatory Temple of the Holy Family represented faith and obedience in purest form. At least, it was meant to. And so, by transference, did Gaudí, whom the Tragic Week turned into a legendary figure in his lifetime, a walking emblem of penitence and devotion.

Lay associations had sprung up like mushrooms in Europe, and particularly in Spain, to propagate the cult of obedience to the infallible pope, Pius IX, who had infallibly defined his own infallibility as a dogma, binding on all the faithful under pain of mortal sin, and therefore, of condemnation to hell.

The chief of these associations in Catalunya called itself the Josephines. They first met at Montserrat, the holy mountain of the Black Virgin, in 1866. They chose a reactionary quartet as honorary patrons, Pius IX, the future king Alfonso XIII, Queen María Cristina, and a soon-to-be-beatified Catalan priest named Antoni Claret. The actual, or managing, leader of the Josephines was a bookseller and amateur flutist named Josep Bocabella i Verdaguer (no relation to the great Catalan poet). Bocabella, it seems, knew very little about architecture. At first the expiatory temple was assigned to a pious mediocrity named Villar, who did Gothic Revival designs. But Villar resigned the next year, 1883, and in 1884 the Josephines found another architect: Antoni Gaudí. Why he was selected remains something of a mystery. He had built very little, and none of his major works, at that time, existed. There is a persistent story, probably too good to be true, that Gaudí got the job because he had such clear, ice blue eyes. One of Bocabella's religious visions had been that the Sagrada Família would be designed by a true Aryan, a man with blue eyes.

Whatever the case, Gaudí had a completely free hand from the moment the Josephines hired him. But no architect can live on the proceeds of a single building, unless he is designing something like the Getty Center, which the Sagrada Família was not. Especially this is so if the building is a church sponsored by a near-penniless organization. Hence the aura of saintly poverty in which Gaudí's name is still enveloped. In the latter years of his life, the old man used literally to beg for funds, knocking on the doors of the wealthy in Sarrià and along the Passeig de Gràcia. No doubt the sight of his close-cropped white poll and shabby black suit struck fear into the bones families of the city. *"Fets aquest sacrifici,"* he would demand. "Make this sacrifice." "Oh no, Señor Gaudí," the target would protest, fishing out a couple of duros, "Really it's no sacrifice at all, believe me." "Then *make* it a sacrifice," the implacable old man would insist. "Sometimes a gift is not a sacrifice. Sometimes it is nothing but vanity. Be sure."

Such legends are much to the taste of Japanese tourists. No question, Gaudí's most devoted fans are Japanese. They perceive Gaudí-san as a sort of Zen samurai, a heroic failure but a man of immeasurable and transcendent moral force.

Droves of young Japanese, mainly architecture students, come to seek work on the Sagrada Família, as pious girls used to flock to Calcutta to wash ulcers and wind bandages for Mother Teresa. They hope, as one of them put it to me as he struggled with a fiberglass cast of a finial, to "absorb the holy message" of the architect. The irony, of course, is that nobody knows in detail what Gaudí's conception was. His drawings were all lost or destroyed seventy years ago in the civil war, a point about which the Gaudíans incessantly lie. Since Gaudí's death there has been no "real" Sagrada Família.

There will never be another Gaudí. Nor is there at all likely to be another state of mind—not in Spain, anyway—resembling the ultraregionalist idea of the creative spirit that determined his work. And one can predict with some confidence that there will not soon be another figure like Gaudí's spiritual adviser, the bishop of Vic, Josep Torras i Bagès, that strange ultranationalist Catholic, rotund, blind as a bat behind his moony pebble lenses, voluble as Ramón Llull and utterly incapable of doctrinal compromise.

Barcelona has changed too much to produce such people and, despite the extreme conservatism of Pope John Paul II, so has the Catholic Church—one hopes. The present pope has made more saints in twenty-five years than any pope in history; it remains to be seen whether the conservative-nationalist elements in the Catalan clergy will prevail upon him to canonize Gaudí. The art of painting has a patron saint, an eminent one: the Apostle Luke, no less. Architecture has none. Perhaps it should have one, for then, as one Catalan delirious at the prospect observed, "It would be such a beautiful thing: Everyone will want to be an architect." But then, perhaps not: The currency of sainthood is worn and shabby today, particularly since John Paul II, to the world's amazement, recently canonized a Mexican, Juan Diego, for whose very existence—never mind personal sanctity—there is not one shred, jot, or tittle of evidence.

Gaudí existed without a doubt, but it would be ridiculous to expect to see a "tradition" of architectural design stemming from him. Any new building related to Gaudí is automatically fated to look like mere imitation. Yet there is no doubt that Gaudí, by focusing modern attention specifically on Catalan architecture (rather than on music, painting, or poetry) made it the emblematic art form of Barcelona after his death. This distinction turned out to be of special importance in the late eighties when Barcelona was designated the host city for the 1992 Olympic Games.

Olympiads generally come and go amid a lot of blather about how they help remake the host city, lift it into permanent world attention, and so on. It is rarely true. Architecturally, neither Melbourne nor Sydney was much better off for the 1956 and 2000 Olympic Games. The years 1976 and 1996 left nothing of memorable quality in Montreal or banal Atlanta.

But the approach of the 1992 Olympiad was the cue for Barcelona to launch the biggest program of excavation and construction, rerouting and reconstruction, cleaning, restoration, and general urban rethinking the city had experienced in a hundred years, since the construction of the Eixample. It was an upheaval in the course of which the city government cunningly used national funds to pay for local changes that were desperately needed but would never normally have been financed by Madrid.

It would take a longish book (and has produced dozens, mostly published in a spirit of relentless self-admiration by the Ajuntament) to detail and describe the changes in the city's fabric this entailed. They run all the way from bylaw codes on the preservation of vintage art nouveau street lettering to the construction of huge arterial highways like the Ronda de Dalt above the city and the Ronda del Litoral along the coast. A stretch of waterfront several kilometers long, running north of the city, which was once a wilderness of rusting tracks and abandoned industrial equipment backing a sea strip nobody visited, has been cleaned out, razed, and turned into a handsome beach side: from dump to prime real estate in a single fiat.

The old Barcelona grisa, gray Barcelona, had performed some truly execrable feats of reverse urbanism; the tract from the Ramblas to Barceloneta had been run-down and almost a slum in places, but now the city government, under the guidance of architect Oriol Bohigas, made it a promenade of elegance, the reenvisioned Moll de la Fusta. The only serious loss to the waterfront (and it is serious, indeed) has been the loss of the *guinetes,* those charming, rickety restaurants on stilts that wandered down the sand and into the sea, where one ate such sublime *parilladas* and paellas, bowls of *sopa de mariscos* and plates of those weird-looking, delicious *percebes* or gooseneck barnacles—plates which can be had in their full quality elsewhere in Barcelona today but which seemed to gain a special savor as the blue fumes of oil and the garlic-heavy scent of *allioli* mingled with the impure sea breezes off the port.

Those in charge of new building in Barcelona did not feel confined to using only Catalan architects. Thus, the enormous new communications tower that shoots up some six hundred feet from the ridge of Collserola behind the city, a splendid and glittering affair of parabolic steel antennas sprouting from a core trunk of concrete, is the work of the British architect Norman Foster. The powerful dome of the stadium, Palau Sant Jordi, now Barcelona's chief venue for indoor sports, was designed by the Japanese Arata Isozaki. These and other Olympic installations by foreigners have continued to serve the city very well.

Less admirable were other projects. Pasqual Maragall, descendant of the great Catalan poet and then mayor of Barcelona, was not immune to star ranking, and he hoped to turn the new construction of his city into a serious architectural anthology. To their credit, he and his chief adviser, Oriol Bohigas, did not touch certain trendy architects of the eighties, such as Michael Graves or that Bernini of Disneyland, Robert A. M. Stern. But he was impressed, not unreasonably, by the fame of Richard Meier, who in 1984 had just corralled the very prestigious Pritzker Prize, the closest thing architecture has to a Nobel. Thus Meier was offered the commission to design a new Museu d'Art Contemporani (Museum of Contemporary Art), which would be built in the Raval—an old, dilapidated area behind the Ramblas and the Liceu—as an emblem of future renovation. Alas, Meier's design was an uncharacteristic failure. Perhaps he found it hard to concentrate, with the enormous task of doing the Getty Center weighing on him. The collection of Barcelona's Museum of Contemporary Art was mediocre to begin with, and Meier's building was unkind to the art, badly lit and spatially only barely coherent.

The worst error of commissioning, however, was the redo of the Palau Nacional atop Montjuïc, home of Barcelona's incomparable collection of Romanesque frescoes. It was done by the extremely mannered Italian architect Gae Aulenti, rather more fashionable two decades ago than she is today, and critics—remembering what a rhetorical hash she had made of converting the enormous Musée d'Orsay in Paris—awaited its unveiling with some trepidation. They were not disappointed.

I had a small pre-opening acquaintance with this flashy and overdetailed building, whose chief feature was a huge vaulted oval hall for grand occasions. This time there would be an awarding of cultural prizes, an idea which, not very surprisingly, would not occur in Atlanta or in Sydney when the next Olympiads came around. They were generous, about five million pesetas (fifty thousand dollars) each, and given to outstanding figures in such domains as visual arts, music, and literature. They would be given by the king, Juan Carlos, who was accompanied by his daughters, the elder known as the Infanta and the younger, due to her girth, unkindly nicknamed the Elefanta.

But now a problem arose and it didn't look like it was going away. In the course of stripping and redoing the interior of this late 1920s mammoth of a hall, Aulenti's builders had left the windows open and dozens, scores of pigeons got in. There, nesting among the bulbous brackets—you could see the straw and twigs sticking out—and fluttering invulnerably under the dome, they took up residence and would not be dislodged. The job had to be finished with the birds still inside.

A week before prize day, on a visit to the Ajuntament, I came across Margarita Obiols, wringing her hands in despair. (Margarita's moments of despair are rare and fleeting, but when they come upon her she looks and sounds like the great Judith Anderson as Medea.) What on Earth was the matter? *"Coloms,"* she said, those damn pigeons. They are going to shit on the king and the *infantas,* and we don't know how to get rid of them before the ceremony.

I thought of the Crystal Palace in London, that marvel of Victorian engineering, and how just before its opening in 1854 the same problem had arisen: It was infested with birds, which could not be shot without stray pellets breaking the glass panes. Famously, when Queen Victoria mentioned this problem to the elderly duke of Wellington, he had replied, "Sparrow hawks, Ma'am!" But neither sparrow hawks nor any other suitable raptor were to be found among the bird-fancying societies of Barcelona.

We then settled for a second plan, not as good. With a couple of marksmen (I wanted Olympic grade, but we had to settle for ordinary bird-hunting journalists like myself), one would go up into the structure of the dome, inching along the catwalks and ladders, and thus get close enough to the pigeons' roosts to let fly with low-powered air guns, whose pellets, if we missed, would not chip the curlicues of painted plaster. After much scrambling, with our hearts in our mouths (at least, I know mine was) we reached our vantage points high in the dome and settled down, covered in dust and pigeon dung, to knock off the birds. They proved quite easy to hit but amazingly difficult to kill. Pigeons are tougher than you think and, with such weak air guns, you had to score a head shot. After a whole morning the three of us had accounted, if I remember aright, for no more than ten gray bundles of feathers, which spiraled far down to the limestone floor and were promptly scooped up by the workmen below, who took them home, presumably for supper. They must have been hoping for a larger bag.

Tired of this inadequate sport and sneezing violently, we at last called it a day and started back down, leaving the pigeon population of Palau Nacional more or less intact. We had to scramble out through a door which gave onto the outside rim of the dome, high in the sky. A terrible chattering roar and a police helicopter came hovering into view round the flank of the dome, its open door crowded with black-uniformed security men who were themselves bristling with automatic weapons. What they saw, I realized with foreboding, was not a trio of dust-caked journalists with silly .177 popguns. Not at all. It would be three Basque terrorists, getting set to murder the king of Spain and his family.

Somehow, much later, we talked our way out of that predicament, but it was a close call. At the ceremony, no Catalan pigeons had the cheek to fly over the royal dais, so the day was saved. One of the papers, reporting the speech of thanks I had to make to the king in Spanish and then in Catalan on behalf of the prizewinners in the Cultural Olympiad, remarked that I resembled "a shaven Hemingway." The writer cannot have been referring to my prose style, and I cannot believe he meant an allusion to my wretchedly meager powers as a Great White Hunter.

THE WORLD OF GAUDÍ AND TORRAS I BAGÈS IS NOW irretrievably gone and so is the Catalunya they prized. What took it off the map? What disposed of the old Catalan nationalism?

In a word, migration. Up to 1920 or so, Spaniards tended not to move around much within their peninsula. An Andalusian would stay in Andalusia, a Galician in

Galicia. What changed this regional loyalty was the development of some areas that offered more and better work than others. Catalunya, being so industrialized, was dramatically changed by this. During the twentieth century it has been constantly altered by waves of immigration. Barcelona has the largest Catalan population of any Spanish city, of course, and most of these people descend from the massive internal migration Catalunya underwent during the last half of the nineteenth century, when people came flooding in from rural areas, attracted by industrial work. Spain's first industrial proletariat was thus essentially Catalan.

But then in the 1920s, and later during the industrial boom of the 1950s and '60s, hundreds of thousands of other kinds of Spaniards came flooding into Barcelona from Galicia, Murcia, Aragon, Estremadura, and Andalusia. At first they settled in the Raval, that run-down place of poverty and racial mixture behind the Ramblas. They gobbled up existing villages on the fringe of Barcelona, like Santa Coloma de Gramenet. They spilled into outlying areas where nobody, a few years before, had even fancied the city could spread to: Torrent Gornal, Verdum, Bellvitge, La Guineneta, places no tourist had seen or heard of. They filled Barcelona with smells and colors it had not known before, not all of them benign in their implications.

On the most obvious level immigration, especially from the Middle East just across the salt water, brought an explosion of street crime and a nightmare of hard drugs, which Catalans invariably blamed on the hated *xarnegos,* the dirty wog foreigners.

Barcelona is a very big city, about four million people, and getting bigger every day. With more Catalans than any other place in Spain it also has the second largest Andalusian population; and so on, down the lines of difference. (The Andalusian Feria de Abril in Barcelona brings together hundreds of thousands of north-living southerners to drink *fino* and play flamenco.)

The social effects of this migratory influx are completely irreversible. Barcelona, a century ago a stiffly exclusive place when it came to perceptions of nationality and culture, is now almost totally and, much of the time, proudly multicultural—more so, perhaps, than any Spanish city except Madrid. There is no blood and race definition of who is and isn't a Catalan. The mere fact of being Catalan confers no rights or privileges in Catalunya. The legal definition is very broad: "The political condition of Catalan" belongs to all Spanish citizens with "administrative residence" in Catalunya. This would have seemed absurdly permissive to Gaudí.

No question, Catalans are still extremely proud of being Catalan. But the signatures of difference have shifted, slowly but inevitably.

For instance, Torras i Bagès and many other conservatives a hundred years ago thought it verged on impropriety for a Catalan to show extreme enthusiasm for bullfighting. The corrida, they supposed, was an "African," unchristian spectacle fit only for moros. Instead, the good Catalan should reserve his highest enthusiasm for the local *castellers*. The *castell* is a human pyramid, formed by muscular *xiquets*—local lads from one's village or home district—standing on one another's shoulders in a series of rings, its apex created by a young, light-bodied boy who manages to scramble up the structure and stand, swaying triumphantly, on top. It was always one of the most popular folk-sport, team-effort demonstrations of equilibrium and cooperation in Spanish life, a proof of the seny traditionally prized as a Catalan virtue.

Catalunya still has its castellers, and delightful they are to see in competition, but the great binding sport of the place is neither castells nor, obviously, bullfighting (though the city has two bullrings) but something it shares with all the rest of Spain—an unquenchable passion for *fútbol*. The Fútbol Club Barcelona (Barcelona Football Club) was founded in

1899 by a Swiss enthusiast and in the following century it ramified with barely credible fecundity, becoming the most extreme and powerful example of Barcelona's mania for clubs and every sort of collective activity, from folk song to pigeon fancying.

The Barcelona Football Club—Barça for short—has its home field in the Camp Nou, "new field," a sports stadium that can easily hold 100,000, built just off the great artery of the Diagonal in 1957. Its home colors are scarlet and navy blue, a heraldry which by now probably equals the traditional quatres barres, the four red bars of Wilfred the Hairy's gore imprinted by Louis the Pious's fingers on their yellow ground, in the city's affections. Its war cry, in all its commendable simplicity, is *Barça! Barça! Barçaaaaa!,* and its club song, written in 1974, is close to being a national anthem, but one for a nation of immigrants rather than valley dwellers:

> *Who cares where we come from,*
> *North or south,*
> *We all agree, we all agree,*
> *One flag makes us brothers.*

With reason, Catalans think of Barcelona as the most interesting city in Spain. But very few of them imagine they get some peculiar moral advantage by living there. Barcelona has now become a genuinely multicultural city, without the woozy overtones (or the odor of mediocrity, slight but unmistakable) that the word "multicultural" has acquired in the United States. It does not find all its cultural traits equally to its taste. The city is even capable of being a bit embarrassed about some of them, as well it might be, particularly now that Barcelona is being promoted by eager American journalists as the newest, hottest thing in European destinations. But no matter. The city may not transcend its faults, but it does outweigh them. Perhaps it always has. "You are boastful and treacherous and vulgar," wrote Joan Maragall, in the last lines of his "Ode to Barcelona." But then, the cry of infatuated loyalty. "Barcelona! And with your sins, ours, ours! Our Barcelona, the great enchantress!" There is still ample truth in this.

IN THE SPRING OF 2003, DORIS HELD HER FIRST ONE-PERSON show. It consisted of botanical watercolors, a subject and medium in which she excels. It was held in an old and respected gallery, the Sala Pares, in the *casc antic* or medieval part of Barcelona, a few minutes' walk from the Ajuntament where we had been married two Christmases, a little more than a year, before.

We flew from New York in coach, the plane packed like a tuna can: an ordeal for a 64-year-old man with a right leg still not healed from the five fractures it had sustained in an auto accident four years earlier. But the prospect of getting to Barcelona made that unimportant. What did matter was that once again I was off to my favorite city in Europe, or the world. For the twentieth time? The thirtieth? Long ago, I lost count.

You are lucky if, not too late in life, you discover a city other than your birthplace which becomes a true hometown. You may not think of your birthplace as your hometown. Certainly I don't think of Sydney that way. I would be sad not to see its blue, many-lobed harbor again, but I know (insofar as anyone can see the future through the prism of desire) that I shall never live there, that returning there forever would be neither an adventure nor a fulfillment. It is too far away, at least from me. Why should patriotism have been fixed for you when you were a fetus? I claim the right to choose what I love, and that includes cities. You may not wish to repudiate your origins (certainly I don't), but you must embrace what you prefer. Forty years ago I had that marvelous stroke of luck: Barcelona and, better still, an unending introduction to that place by people who are still my dear friends.

Wiped out by the flight, and hoping to catch a few hours' sleep before Saturday lunch (which would wipe us out again, and send us down to a deeper level of rest before dinner with Xavier Corberó, whose baby eels with dried red peppers in boiling oil and subsequent paella would at last weigh us down into full unconsciousness), Doris and I collapsed in our room in the Hotel Colon, overlooking the Cathedral square. Colon is the Catalan name of Columbus. Many Catalans firmly believe, as an article of faith almost, that Christopher Columbus really was Catalan, not Genoese: a notion for which there is not a crumb of evidence, though that has never dissuaded Catalans from believing anything they think will redound to their fame and glory. After all, many Catalans are also quite sure that it was some nameless compatriot of theirs who, centuries ago, became the first person in the whole wide world to rub a cut ripe tomato on a slice of bread, thereby creating the *pa amb tomaquet,* which is such a staple of the Catalan table; and next to discovering a dish as fundamental as this, discovering America is not such a transcendental deal.

We slept. Bright buttery patches of morning sun crept across the carpet. Very gradually we were woken by music floating up from the Cathedral square. Not the aggressive grating of rock radio, still less the degenerate thump and jabber of rap (a favorite now with Catalan teenies). It crept into the room with extraordinary sweetness, repetitive yet subtly varied.

Oboes and cornets, no strings, nothing amplified. "Be not afeard: this isle is full of noises / Sounds and sweet airs, that give delight, and hurt not." The Catalans were dancing their national dance, the *sardana.* They had spontaneously formed rings of eight, ten, as many as twenty people, holding hands. In the middle of each ring was a little pile of coats, hats, shopping baskets, set down on the cobbles so that all the dancers could keep an eye on their things.

Their movements were stately and minimal. They did not prance; they shuffled, so that the old ones could keep up with the young. What the sardana declares is cooperation. It is a citizenship dance. It does not highlight individual virtuosity, still less egotism. (If you want those, the Cathedral square is usually zipping with skateboards.) It includes children and teenagers, the old and gray, the slow, the lame, the fat and the whippet thin, the elegant and the dowdy. It brings families and friends together, in sweetness, without a trace of irony. It is a perfect expression of shared goodwill, and lovely to watch. We watched, with delight. Doris and I felt very far from New York City, and we were.

ABOUT THE AUTHOR

ROBERT HUGHES has been an art critic for *Time* magazine since 1970. He is the author of many books, including the bestselling *Fatal Shore,* as well as the originator and narrator of the highly acclaimed PBS television series *The Shock of the New, American Visions,* and *Australia: Beyond the Fatal Shore.* A frequent contributor to *The New York Review of Books,* Hughes lives in New York City.

This book is set in Garamond 3, designed by Morris
Fuller Benton and Thomas Maitland Cleland in the
1930s, released digitally by Adobe; and selected
faces of the Priori family, inspired by British typog-
raphy of the early twentieth century, designed by
Johnathon Barnbrook, released digitally by
Emigre. The dings are Woodtype Ornaments,
designed by Barbara Lind and Joy Redick, released
digitally by Adobe.

Printed by R. R. Donnelley and Sons on
Gladfelter 60-pound Thor Offset smooth
white antique paper.

Dust jacket printed by Miken Companies.
Color separation by Quad Graphics.

Three-piece case of Ecological Fiber bamboo side
panels with Sierra black book cloth as the spine
fabric. Stamped in Lustrofoil metallic silver.

OTHER TITLES IN THE SERIES

JAN MORRIS *A Writer's House in Wales*

OLIVER SACKS *Oaxaca Journal*

W. S. MERWIN *The Mays of Ventadorn*

WILLIAM KITTREDGE *Southwestern Homelands*

DAVID MAMET *South of the Northeast Kingdom*

GARRY WILLS *Mr. Jefferson's University*

A. M. HOMES *Los Angeles: People, Places, and the Castle on the Hill*

JOHN EDGAR WIDEMAN *The Island: Martinique*

FRANCINE PROSE *Sicilian Odyssey*

SUSANNA MOORE *I Myself Have Seen It: The Myth of Hawai'i*

LOUISE ERDRICH *Book and Islands in Ojibwe Country*

KATHRYN HARRISON *The Road to Santiago*

ARIEL DORFMAN *Desert Memories: Journeys Through the Chilean North*

BARRY UNSWORTH *Crete*

HOWARD NORMAN *My Famous Evening: Nova Scotia Sojourns, Diaries & Preoccupations*

UPCOMING AUTHORS

ANNA QUINDLEN *on London*

JAMAICA KINCAID *on Nepal*

DIANE JOHNSON *on Paris*

GEOFFREY WOLFF *on Maine*

JON LEE ANDERSON *on Andalucia*

WILLIAM LEAST HEAT-MOON *on Western Ireland*